YOU'RE HIRED!

INTERVIEW ANSWERS

YOU'RE HIRED! INTERVIEW ANSWERS

IMPRESSIVE ANSWERS TO TOUGH QUESTIONS

CERI RODERICK AND STEPHAN LUCKS

You're Hired! Interview Answers: Impressive answers to tough questions

This edition first published in 2010 by Trotman Publishing, a division of Crimson Publishing Ltd., Westminster House, Kew Road, Richmond, Surrey TW9 2ND

© Trotman 2010

Authors Ceri Roderick and Stephan Lucks

British Library Cataloguing in Publication Data
A catalogue record for this book is available from the British Library

ISBN 978 1 84455 229 0

Printed and bound in Great Britain by TJ International Ltd, Padstow, Cornwall

Acknowledgements

With thanks to our clients and colleagues with whom we gained the valuable experience to write this book.

CONTENTS

LIST OF ACTIVITIES

ABOUT THE AUTHORS

Ceri Roderick is a Partner and Head of Assessment at business psychologists Pearn Kandola, and has been designing and delivering tough interviews for over 20 years. After a period with Deloittes, he joined Pearn Kandola in 2000, working with blue chip companies and government departments, nationally and internationally, on all aspects of assessment.

Stephan Lucks is a Managing Psychologist at Pearn Kandola where he specialises in the design and implementation of assessment and development processes for organisations, management and senior management development, and one-to-one coaching. He is a Chartered Occupational Psychologist with over 17 years experience.

INTRODUCTION

The prospect of going for any interview can be pretty daunting, even more so if it is a process that is billed as a 'tough' interview. Images of being grilled by a relentless interviewer come to mind, but in fact, when they are done well, interviews are not intended to be deliberately intimidating, or designed to trip you up; they are simply designed to be very thorough. The plus side is that if you handle them well they give you the best opportunity to show yourself in a good light. This book is designed to make sure that you do handle them well, and by following our guidance and tips you'll be well armed to face the toughest of interviews.

We have deliberately aimed this book at graduates, middle and senior management roles, as people in this bracket are most likely to experience this type of interview. Overall, it will be of use to anybody seeking a professional role in an organisation.

This book is about a very particular type of interview – the structured competency-based interview. Experienced recruiters use them a lot, and they are probably the toughest interviews you will come across. With the right knowledge, preparation and work experience, though, you can actually turn the situation around and make it the most straightforward interview you have. We'll explain how in more detail later, but for now rest assured that if you follow the guidance in these pages and you have the appropriate experience, then going for this type of interview is not going to be intimidating. On the contrary, you're more likely to do well and get the job you want.

So, this book will provide you a rich resource to help you prepare for that job-winning interview. Whilst it will introduce you to a very specific type of interview, the approaches and techniques presented here will stand you in good stead in any interview situation, giving you the chance to manage it in a way that demonstrates your skills and abilities.

How to navigate this book

Although this book is written in a serial fashion and can take you from beginning to end in your preparation, it doesn't have to be read that way. It's OK to just dip in and out of it – if you have interview experience you may know exactly what area you want to focus on, and want to turn straight to that.

In a nutshell, here is an outline of what is covered:

Chapter 1: What is a competency and what is a competency-based interview?

The really tough interviews are those that test your relevant work experience, skills and aptitudes. These are called competency-based interviews. If you're not familiar with this approach, this chapter will introduce you to the concept of competencies, giving you a shorthand way of understanding different competencies more easily and explaining how, in an interview, these are tested and explored.

Chapter 2: Preparing for the interview

In this chapter you'll learn about all the different ways in which you need to prepare yourself for the interview. There's guidance about sources of preparatory information and the different aspects of preparation. If you already understand all about competency-based interviews you may want to start here.

Chapter 3: During the interview

Clearly, how you conduct yourself in the interview is important, but equally important is how you respond and structure your responses; this will have a big impact on how well you come across and, consequently, how well you do. This chapter is packed with hints and tips about how you can achieve this and actually manage the interview in a way that shows you in the best light possible. You may have all the right attributes, but you have to get them out there, where the interviewer can see them.

Chapters 4 to 6

These three chapters deal with the three broad competency areas outlined in Chapter 1. This is the section of the book where we share a range of questions and what effective and less-effective answers look like. We're not giving you the answers – that wouldn't be possible – but by working with the structure from Chapter 1 and giving you examples of what a strong or weak response would look like in practice, we aim to help you hone your answering technique so that you get the best out of the question. The key here is to see the questions as opportunities and not as traps!

Chapter 7: Non-competency-based questions – but still tough!

Even though an interview may be signposted as a competency-based interview, you can never be sure that the interviewer won't throw in questions that are not strictly competency based. You can't avoid them when this happens, so this chapter addresses how you can respond to these types of question, again giving you examples.

Chapter 8: Troubleshooting/FAQ

Finally, this chapter is a quick reference guide. It addresses the most common questions you may have and provides you with further potential sources of information.

The book will not blind you with science, but inevitably there will be some places where we need to draw on and explain the science behind this particular way of interviewing so that you are well informed about the process. The good part is that whilst it is headlined as 'Answering tough interview questions', there is a real reason why organisations use this approach – it helps them choose the best people for the job, but it also gives you the best opportunity to show how good you are. So whilst it may be tough, it's actually doing you a favour and ensuring that if you get the job you are going for, you will probably be a good fit, which in turn means you're likely to perform well and enjoy it more than if you were less well adapted to the role.

Apart from learning about being interviewed and getting lots of hints and tips throughout, what you'll also gain is the eye of a critical consumer. The interview is a great window on an organisation and gives you a good opportunity to evaluate the company and whether you want to work there. It's always important to remember that an interview is a two-way process, and a good interviewer will also be aware of this. They will be trying to sell their organisation to you. What they may not be aware of, though, is that the selection process in itself will also communicate something to you. By learning about good interviewing technique, you'll be in a better position to evaluate whether an organisation's processes are fair, thorough and relevant to the job that you are going for. We know from our own work that candidates are most likely to trust a selection decision based on a process that they see as tough, testing and well managed.

The key message to leave you with, therefore, is not to be fearful of this type of interview. Reading this book and adhering to the guidance we provide here will put you in a powerful position to do well at interview, and help you in getting the job you really desire.

1 WHAT IS A COMPETENCY AND WHAT IS A COMPETENCY-BASED INTERVIEW?

This chapter is going to be a vital starting point if you have no knowledge or previous experience of this type of interview. In it you'll discover:

■ what competencies are

■ what the interview process is and how an interviewer will structure the interview

■ how competencies can be grouped into three easy-to-remember categories that will help you in your preparation.

Exploring competencies

You may well have come across the term 'competencies' before. Most organisations refer to competencies, but what exactly are they and how are they useful? Understanding how and why competencies are used will help you to focus your preparation and perform your best at interview.

Put simply, competencies are the way that organisations define the qualities that they need (and that you need) to be excellent at a job. Not to be confused with skills, competencies are usually concerned with *how* we do things, whereas skills are usually about *what* we do. Think of competencies as the adjectives of skills. To give you a concrete example:

- 'Producing accounts' is a skill. It is a specific set of steps and procedures.
- 'Providing information in a timely and accurate manner' is a competency. The 'timely' and 'accurate' descriptors – the *how* bit – make this a competency. So, competencies are the behaviours which are used to exercise a skill.

Competencies are usually concerned with how *we do things; skills are usually about* what *we do.*

When using them for recruitment and performance measurement, businesses need competencies to be specific enough to be recognisable by people, but general enough that they can be applied across a range of jobs in the organisation. So, coming back to our example above, 'Producing accounts in a timely and accurate manner' is very specific; it applies only to people working in an accounts role, and would be inappropriate in, say, a research and development role. However, 'Providing information in a timely and accurate manner' can apply to both roles – and probably a lot of others as well.

Competencies are typically drawn together in what is known as a 'competency model'. A competency model is simply a collection of competencies which define what outstanding performance would look like. Typically, organisations have between seven to nine competencies, although of course some organisations have many more.

Let's take a look at some competencies:

- planning and organising
- creativity and innovation
- team leadership
- achievement orientation
- analytical thinking
- influencing and persuading
- energy and drive
- judgement and decision making
- motivating others.

The nine competencies listed above are typical of those that organisations use and could be applied to a wide range of different jobs. Competencies that you may have come across may well have different names to those listed above, because competencies in part describe the nature and culture of an organisation and, quite rightly, organisations hone the wording to reflect their specific needs. In this sense, the competency framework is an important way in which an organisation differentiates itself and makes clear – for itself and for others – 'what it is you have to do to be effective around here'. So, while specific wording will vary, the nine competencies outlined above are a good generic 'average' of the kinds of competency you will see, and they fit a lot of organisations.

A lot of work has been done on job analysis and on statistically analysing organisational behaviours to identify what it is that differentiates good performance in any specific job. Look at most competency models, and they can be collapsed (or clustered) into three broad areas. This gives you a very useful shorthand for understanding the competencies of an organisation. The three areas are:

- **Task competencies:** these are about delivering/completing tasks, setting objectives, getting things done.
- **Thought competencies:** these are typically about direction, strategy, creativity, problem solving, change, innovation, judgement, decision making.
- **People competencies:** these are about the people things, communicating, motivating, developing.

As you can see from this list, almost all jobs will require elements from each of these three areas. For example, very few jobs are purely about task delivery – there are bound to be 'people' and 'thought' elements involved. In the same way, very few jobs would allow you to focus on 'thought' to the exclusion of all else; it's highly likely you will have to talk to people and deliver something too!

We have clustered the example competencies here into the task, thought and people categories:

Task	Thought	People
Energy and drive	Judgement and decision making	Motivating others
Achievement orientation	Analytical thinking	Influencing and persuading
Planning and organising	Creativity and innovation	Team leadership

We call this model the Leadership Radar™, because, like steering a ship or flying a plane, you need to keep your eye on all the radar screens if you want to navigate a safe course. Sometimes you'll need to focus on just one screen, at other times all three screens need to be taken into account. We'll return to this model in Chapter 2 and show you how you can use it to make a success of interviews, for example by using it to simplify your preparation.

Structured competency-based interviews

Not all interviews are the same, and not all interviews are equally effective in uncovering relevant information on which to base a selection decision. For a long time – and for some organisations this includes the present – interviews focused on work history, some general questions about what you were interested in, why you wanted to work for the organisation and so on. Such unstructured interviews, often conducted without there being any clear criteria in mind, did little more than give the interviewer some general idea about your social confidence and verbal fluency and 'whether they liked the look of you'. Research showed that such interviews operated at little better than chance levels in terms of picking the right person for the job. In a lot of cases, the organisation would have done just as well by selecting CVs at random. There is a joke in the HR profession that you could just throw the pile of CVs in the air, and the ones that landed face up got invited to interview. (It *is* a joke, and we know of no one actually doing this!)

A structured, competency-based interview is intended to counter this impressionistic approach and is designed around three core premises:

- past behaviour is a good predictor of future behaviour
- competencies are a good indicator of success at a job
- maintaining a structure and asking each candidate the same questions ensures that you can more systematically differentiate between candidates in terms of relevant criteria.

Let's look at each of these in turn.

Past behaviour is a good predictor of future behaviour

Research has indeed shown that what people do and how they do it is relatively consistent over time. Past behaviour is therefore a good predictor of future behaviour. That is not to say that people cannot learn and develop over time, and a good interview will explore your learning as well – particularly when the job represents a step up from previous roles or involves different kinds of work. In general terms, however, if you can provide lots of rich examples of how you have structured and planned tasks, the interviewer can increase their confidence that this is an approach that you regularly adopt and that you will therefore bring it to this job as well.

Competencies are a good indicator of success at a job

Again, research has shown a relationship between how well somebody's competencies are developed and how successfully they perform their role. So, for example, people who score poorly on 'focusing on customers' in an interview also tend not to perform well on this in a job. The interviewer's task is to explore each competency thoroughly enough to be able to give a confident rating of your likely performance in relation to that competency. So, what you are good at is a fairly obvious indicator of your performance in a job that involves that skill, but at the same time the interviewer has to be satisfied that you really do have that competency.

Maintaining a structure and asking each candidate the same questions ensures that you can more systematically differentiate between candidates

This one is quite logical really. If you do not ask questions about the same competencies of all candidates that are being interviewed, you will not have all of the information that is needed to make a good hiring decision. There is no point exploring one person's people management skills and another person's organisational skills only. You won't be able to differentiate between the two. The structure also ensures that nothing is left out and that all areas are explored in sufficient depth. Once again, the interviewer's job is to pursue a particular line of enquiry until they are satisfied that they can give you an accurate rating.

IDENTIFYING COMPETENCY-BASED QUESTIONS

Have a look at the questions below and see if you can identify the structured competency-based questions:

1. 'Describe to me a time where you helped a member of your team to improve their performance.'
2. 'What sort of people management experience do you have?'
3. 'One of your team is not performing as well as they need to be. What would you do?'

Of the three questions above, only 1 is a true, structured competency-based question.

Question 2 is quite generic and is not designed to elicit specific past behaviour. It invites the candidate to describe their approach, and of course has the risk that they will decide to describe only the positive aspects of their style, or give you a textbook answer that does not represent what they are actually capable of doing.

Question 3 is what we would call a situational question. It presents you with a situation and asks what you would do. Again, it does not test what you have actually done – it asks what you would do, hypothetically. People who are quick witted, and fast on their feet can answer this kind of question well; the trouble is, you are then measuring how well they can answer questions and not how well they can actually deliver the competency. We could give you a very plausible theoretical answer to a question about how we would resuscitate someone after a heart attack – we've watched enough episodes of *Casualty* – but we have never done it, nor would you want us practising on you!

What is the structure and process of the interview?

There are two key components to a well conducted interview: the structure/ process and the questioning technique. The interviewer will often use a process called the funnel technique, where, essentially, he or she will funnel and probe more and more to gather very specific details about what you did in a particular situation.

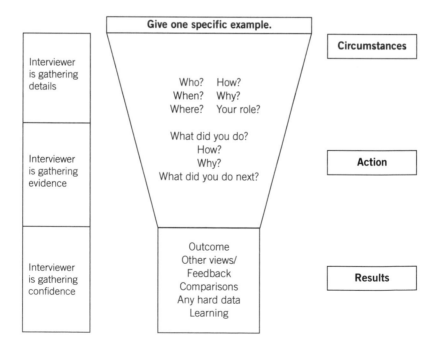

	Give one specific example.	
		Circumstances
Interviewer is gathering details	Who? How? When? Why? Where? Your role?	
Interviewer is gathering evidence	What did you do? How? Why? What did you do next?	**Action**
Interviewer is gathering confidence	Outcome Other views/ Feedback Comparisons Any hard data Learning	**Results**

As you can see from the funnel technique diagram, the interviewer will start with a broad question designed to elicit a specific example. E.g. 'Describe to me a time where you helped a member of your team to improve their performance.'

Following this, the interviewer will gather further details, such as the circumstances, who was involved, when this was, where, what your role was and why were you involved. The interviewer will then move on to gathering information about what you did – your actions, why you did them, and what other options you considered. They will want a step-by-step run-through of what you did.

Finally, the interviewer will want to know about the outcome or results of the situation. What sort of feedback did you get, what hard data have you got about the outcome, what did you learn, would you do anything differently if faced with a similar situation?

All of this is summarised by the **CAR** acronym on the right of the diagram. It's important to remember this and to have it at the back of your mind for every interview. Framing your answers in these terms will help the interviewer to focus more quickly on the positive attributes you want to get across.

- **C**ircumstances
- **A**ction
- **R**esults

You can imagine that with this level of questioning and probing, it's going to be difficult to make something up in the spur of the moment. And with all of this probing, the interviewer is not only collecting details of what you have done, they are also building confidence that you are being truthful in your responses.

It is this structure, the probing and the seeking of real examples of activity, that differentiates the competency-based approach from the more traditional interview process. Please believe us, that it is very difficult to invent answers in this situation – it shows! What you can do, based on familiarity with the structure, is prepare and present your examples in a way which helps the interviewer. This will also help you!

THE RECRUITMENT PROCESS

You can encounter an interview at various stages of the recruitment process:

- as an initial screening method before being asked to come back for another form of assessment
- as part of a longer day where different tools are used, e.g. psychometric tests, written exercises, or a role-play
- during an assessment centre – similar to above, but typically more in depth and making use of group discussions, simulated meetings and written exercises
- as the very last stage before a final decision is made.

How will the interview be conducted?

Some companies will have a single interviewer, whilst others are likely to use two. Whilst this may at first seem intimidating, it is actually doing you a favour. Best practice is to use two interviewers, as it is a demanding job and taking notes whilst interviewing can be very difficult. Splitting the workload, therefore, makes it a more accurate and reliable process and reduces the chance of error creeping in.

Other organisations use a panel of interviewers. This is particularly popular in public sector organisations. Panels are typically made up of between three and five people representing different departments or interested parties. There may also be an HR representative in the interview. In a panel, there will usually be one person who chairs the process and the others will ask the questions. It is usually a very formal process and from that point of view can be more intimidating, but the intention is the same as with a non-panel format.

A final way that an interview may be conducted is over the telephone or using technology such as video conferencing. This approach is likely to be used if a role requires a lot of telephone interaction, such as a telesales position, or if, for logistical reasons, it is not possible to have a face-to-face interview. If applying for a role that has an international dimension, for example, you may well have an interview using video conferencing technology with interested parties who are unable to attend in person.

Finally, of course, the number of interviews you face may vary. Some organisations will use several interviews to start filtering down from many applicants to just a preferred few. Yet others will conduct several interviews, with each interview focusing on just one or two competencies rather than on all at one go. This is becoming more popular with more senior roles, as the complexity of the job being applied for can make it difficult to explore everything at once – unless of course they were to interview you for several hours at a time!

Whatever the format of the interview, or whatever stage of the selection process it is being used, the same principles apply in terms of how to conduct yourself and make sure that you present yourself as well as possible.

Why are competency-based interviews used at all?

Competency-based interviews work better for the organisation, even though they require more effort, training and preparation on the part of the interviewer. Businesses wouldn't bother if there wasn't a pay-off – and there is one. At the same time there is also a pay-off for you as the candidate.

The table below shows how well different types of assessment methods are able to predict later job performance. For those who are not statistically minded, the numbers in the second column are what are known as correlation coefficients and they are a measure, in this instance, of the validity of a selection process. In other words, they show the relationship between performance in one situation and performance in another. Correlation coefficients can range between -1 and +1, with a value of 0 indicating no correlation, a value of -1 meaning perfect negative correlation and +1 meaning perfect positive correlation. The higher the number, therefore, the better the validity or predictive power of the tool. (To illustrate the significance of this we've included tossing a coin, which has a correlation of 0.)

Method	Validity
Psychometric (ability) tests	0.5
Assessment centres	0.5
Structured interview	0.4
Competency interview (past behaviour)	0.4
Situational interview	0.3
Unstructured Interview	0.3
Graphology	0.02
Tossing a coin	0

Structured interviews and competency-based interviews are among those with the highest correlations. So, competency-based interviews are used because they let an employer make a better prediction of how well someone is likely to perform in a job.

However, their ability to facilitate better selection decisions is not the only reason why organisations use structured competency-based interviews. Employment legislation is now such that it is incumbent on the employer to be able to demonstrate that their processes are fair, should an applicant call them into question. Structured competency-based interviews are fairer for a number of reasons.

■ The competencies tested are relevant to the role – asking questions about your people-management skills is clearly relevant to a managerial position. Asking you how you would build a tower with three pieces of rope, a few straws and some sticky tape is not.
■ The process follows the same structure, so all applicants are treated the same – it will generate comparable data.
■ The process creates a clear audit trail that is evidence based.
■ The structure and training reduce the impact of bias and stereotypes – the process is therefore fairer. Again, research has shown that the differences between how different groups of people e.g. men and women, Black and Minority Ethnic (BME) or non-BME perform in this type of interview are fewer than in other types of interview.

The combination of the thoroughness, fairness and validity of the interview is the reason why organisations use them. To put it bluntly, it reduces the chances of making a poor hiring decision (the cost of which is usually about 1.5 times salary, when you consider having to re-advertise and reselect a more suitable person) and reduces the risk of being taken to a tribunal on the grounds of discrimination.

Why should you care about any of this? The answer is that the benefits to the organisation actually hold benefits for you too, as shown in the table below.

Features of the interview	Benefits to you
Valid, it is a good predictor of job performance.	You are being selected on the basis of relevant attributes. Getting a job for which you have the right characteristics will result in higher job satisfaction than if you are accidently selected for one that you are not so good at.
Competencies are linked clearly to the role.	You can see the relevance of the questions, there is no dark art involved – perceived fairness is thus higher.
There is a clear audit trail, notes are taken.	Evidence is available to enable the organisation to provide you with feedback, whether you are successful or not.
Structure ensures all candidates are treated the same.	The process is fair, chances of discrimination are reduced.

So whilst these interviews are tough, in that they really test your capabilities, it's better to be on the receiving end of one of these than of some other, unstructured, open-ended interview. Handled well, they give you a better chance to get your relevant abilities across.

The feedback we get is that people much prefer to get a job after having gone through a tough interview that was conducted professionally, clearly related to the role and fair, than to go through an interview that seemed less thorough, less related to the role and unfair. In the latter, you may end up in a job that you are ill-suited to, or worse, be discriminated against in some way. From our experience we know that job applicants, whilst finding structured interviews tough, are more likely to buy into the decision that is made, be it positive or negative for them. Those who get a job feel that they really have earned it, whilst those who are rejected understand why. The feedback that is given, which is linked to the competencies and therefore to the role, helps them to recognise why they were not suitable and, importantly, provides information that they can use for development purposes. Although you may not feel it at the time, you should, therefore, be pleased if you have been invited to this type of interview, rather than feel daunted by it!

What is the interviewer looking for?

So you now know what a competency is, what a competency-based interview is and why they are a good thing. But what is an interviewer looking for when they ask you all those questions?

Simply, they are exploring your competence to carry out the job/role you have applied for. The interviewer is interested in the evidence that you can provide as to your suitability and, specifically, is looking for concrete examples of things that you have done. They will be asking you to illustrate your experience and skills by talking them through real examples of work activity in your career to date – thus eliciting that evidence of past behaviour that we now know is a good predictor of future performance.

People much prefer to get a job having gone through a tough interview that was conducted professionally.

Remember **CAR**? (See page 15 if you've forgotten.) The interviewer is asking you to provide information about the context of the situation, what you did and what the results were. They are looking for a comprehensive answer that illustrates what you actually did. They are not looking for general answers that illustrate what you might do in theory.

IN A NUTSHELL

In this chapter we have looked at the idea of the competency-based interview and how it differs from a more traditional interview. In summary:

■ Competencies are the qualities that are needed to perform effectively in an organisation.

■ Competencies can be grouped into three broad headings of task-related, thought-related and people-related activities.

■ In its assessment processes, an organisation may use a structured, competency-based interview as a means to assessing whether you have the experience necessary to demonstrate these competencies. Research has shown that this is a good method of assessing competencies – performance in the interview is related to job performance.

2 PREPARING FOR THE INTERVIEW

'Can't I just be myself: I'm qualified for a sales job and surely they will see that?'

We've heard candidates say this, and while 'be yourself' is very good advice, trusting to your native cunning rather than some proper preparation is leaving a lot to chance, especially when you are competing with candidates who have done their homework – and believe us, a lot of them will. In this chapter we will:

■ show you how to research the organisation you are applying to

■ show you how to understand its competencies and selection criteria

■ give you tips on researching the interview situation

■ show you how to prepare yourself.

Perfecting your preparation

Preparing for your interview is essential if you are to have the best chance of giving your best. Not only does preparation help you to anticipate some of the questions you are likely to be asked, it also ensures that you have gathered some basic information about the organisation that you are hoping to join. After all, if you are planning to work for it, you should at least aim to find out if its reputation, its operating style and the way it is likely to use you matches your requirements. From its side, you are unlikely to impress if you can't talk with some understanding about the business, its operating environment and competitors (if private sector) or its main purposes, objectives and services (if public sector). In an ideal world – and particularly for senior level roles – the recruitment process should be one where both parties are trying to make an informed decision about how good the 'match' is. You are only going to be able to take part in this assessment of mutual 'fit' if you have done some homework.

The good news is that it has never been easier – thanks to the internet – to research organisations; the bad news is that you have to assume that all the other interview candidates will do diligent preparation and research as well. So, how do you make yourself stand out?

As a minimum, your preparation should include:

- researching the organisation and/or the department that you are applying to
- finding out as much as you can about its selection criteria/competencies
- finding out as much as you can about the interview process (timing, structure, location, interviewers)
- personal preparation – understanding your assets and risks in relation to the job and preparing yourself mentally.

Researching the organisation/ department

There are several very good reasons for researching the organisation you are seeking to join.

■ So that you know exactly what you are getting into – is this the kind of organisation in which you can prosper; how do your talents match its advertised needs?
■ So that you can ask sensible questions at the end of the interview – you will usually be given the chance, and it is a final opportunity to impress.
■ So that you can anticipate some of the questions you will be asked – what are the key things the organisation is likely to be looking for?
■ So that you can show you are interested in the organisation, motivated to join it and that you have been proactive in investigating its requirements.

It's worth emphasising that most organisations will expect you to have done this research and will be disappointed if it becomes clear that you haven't. Imagine these questions being asked:

■ 'So how much do you know about us?'
■ 'What makes you interested in working for us in particular?'
■ 'What do you see as the main challenges in the role you are applying for?'
■ 'What do you think about our recent press coverage?'

Giving a decent answer to questions like these depends on the research you have done. Even when applying for an internal position, perhaps in a different department, you should still do your basic homework. You have to assume that the person or people interviewing you are enthusiastic, passionate and committed to their business. You need to mirror this if you want to 'get on their wavelength' and impress.

Where to find information

Company website

Clearly, the internet and the organisation's own website should be your first port of call. This will usually give you valuable information about the structure of the organisation, its stated values, its markets and services and the kinds of people it employs in different roles. You may also find reference to the specific job you have applied for; if you do, you should read this very thoroughly, making a note of how the job fits into the wider organisation and any other information about the job role.

Job and person specifications

It is worth being clear about some of the different terminology organisations use to define jobs and the people who do them. Typically, there are two main distinctions to be aware of:

- **Job/role specification**: this usually describes the nature of the role in terms of duties and responsibilities. In other words, regardless of the specific individual doing the job, this is what any job holder would be expected to deliver. A typical example might be 'monitor and control expenditure against department budget'. This doesn't say anything about the attributes needed to do this, it simply describes the duty. If the job/role description is all that is available to you, you need to take the extra step and think about 'what kind of person would they be looking for to do this well'. In other words, you need to produce your own 'person specification'.
- **Person specification**: this goes further than the job specification, to describe the kinds of attributes and skills required to do the job well. A typical example might be 'detail-conscious and accurate in checking figures'.

Sometimes organisations muddle these up and you may need to do some reading between the lines in order to better understand the kind of person the organisation is likely to be looking for, and not just the duties involved in the job. The table on page 28 gives some examples.

Job specification	Person specification
Monitor and control expenditure against department budget.	Detail-conscious and accurate in checking figures.
Produce plans for staff allocation to projects against tight timescales.	Structured thinker who does not become flustered when under pressure.
Implement team objectives in line with department priorities.	Clear communicator who can brief people about what is required and when.
Answer customer calls and deal with any complaints that arise.	Even-tempered and calm when dealing with irate people.

JOB AND PERSON SPECIFICATIONS

Here are some job specifications for you to interpret yourself. Think about the kind of person who would do that part of the job well; what kind of personal characteristics would they have?

Job specification	Person specification
Analyse monthly sales figures and produce summary reports	
Represent the firm at conferences and trade shows	
Conduct annual appraisals and agree annual bonuses	

Remember, this part of your research is all about understanding the job and what it will take to do it well!

Most large organisations will provide a wealth of information online. Typical website headings include:

- **About us**: always read this, it typically contains some company history, information about structure, key people, recent news coverage.

- **Careers**: clearly important, you should read all the relevant information under headings like 'Meet our people', 'Why join us?' as well as looking for definitions of different job roles, job specifications and any overall company values and competencies they provide.
- **Publications**: it is well worth looking at the company report, not just in terms of the organisation's performance (remember, the company report is a PR document!) but also in terms of values, objectives and company culture.

Even small organisations will have websites that include a lot of relevant information.

Other websites

If you put the name of your target organisation into any of the main search engines you will get a lot of other hits in addition to the company's own website. It's worth exploring some of these because they will give you a view of how the business is seen by outsiders. Organisations are all keenly interested in their reputation. By having a sense of how the world sees them you will be much better equipped to give intelligent answers (and ask intelligent questions) during your interview. Wikipedia, market intelligence websites, newspaper sites, consumer sites and profession/trade sites can all provide very useful background. Be nosey, try to understand what makes the organisation tick!

Newspapers and magazines

While these are most likely to be useful for direct information about large organisations, they can also tell you a lot about what is going on in a particular market or sector. So, while a small retailer you are applying to may not get much in the way of regular coverage, the financial pages of the main papers will tell you a lot about the retail climate, which parts of the sector are doing relatively well or badly, and so on. If you are applying to a listed company it is also well worth knowing the current share price and whether its trend is up or down – while you might not drop this information into the interview directly, it will tell you something about the likely mood in the business.

For broad information about trends and wider market factors, *The Economist* is a particularly good source. It conducts regular sector reviews that can give you a strong insight into what is keeping the directors of your target organisation awake at night! A quick look at the trade press section in any large news-agent's can also pay off in terms of background information. An hour spent reading *The Grocer* (retail), *Oil and Gas* (energy sector), *Accountancy Today* (business consulting) and similar journals can go a long way to acquainting you with the issues, the players and the jargon, particularly if you are applying for a job in a sector that is unfamiliar to you.

The organisation itself

Don't hesitate to be pushy in terms of accessing any information that the organisation itself can provide. Check to see if it is willing to send you the competencies or criteria it will be interviewing against; ask if there is anyone you can talk to in order to get a better insight into the job; take advantage of any offer of a visit or a pre-interview briefing. Asking for these things shows that you are keen, and the worst that can happen is that they say no!

Do you already know anyone who works for your target organisation? An informal discussion with an insider can tell you a lot. Failing that, explore any contacts you have with suppliers of your target organisation, or even with its competitors. Again, such people can give you a relatively objective view of the business. For example, a candidate we worked with used a personal contact in a competitor organisation to get just such a 'heads up' on a prospective employer. The insight they gained included the backgrounds of some key members of staff, information about their reputation in the sector and details about a key project that they were currently struggling to deliver. Most of this information was directly applicable to the interview.

At the end of your research, the questions you should be able to answer include the following.

- What are the main business priorities at the moment?
- How are they seen by the competition; by the staff; by the industry?
- What are they famous/infamous for?
- What do they hold up as their big successes or failures?
- What kinds of people get ahead in the organisation?
- How do they compare to or differ from similar organisations?

The more you can find out, the better. As we will see later, this information is not intended to enable you to be a smart alec during the interview; rather, it puts you in a much better position to understand the questions you are being asked and, as a result, to frame better answers.

Understanding their competencies/ criteria: what are they looking for?

In Chapter 1 we looked at a model for understanding and simplifying any organisation's competencies – the 'task, thought, people' model. We can now apply this in order to prepare for different kinds of interview approach and different kinds of questions.

'Task, thought, people'

You will encounter some interviews that are less structured and where the criteria are much less clear. With preparation, you can be in the best possible position to get your strengths across even when the interview process is less than ideal. Your homework in terms of 'what are they looking for' is even more important in this situation, as you may not be able to rely on being questioned in the relevant areas. The 'task, thought, people' model is particularly powerful here. Even if the organisation does not have (or is not willing to share) its competencies/criteria, it will be looking for attributes that cluster under these headings. Using the 'task, thought, people' model as part of your preparation, you can present information in a way that they will find easy to identify and digest. By using the model, you will give more rounded, more complete answers, even when questions are not particularly well framed. For more on this, see Chapter 7, on 'non-competency-based questions'.

Remember:
- **Task competencies**: typically about operational delivery, results, implementation, plans, targets, getting things done.
- **Thought competencies**: typically about direction, strategy, creativity, problem solving, change, innovation, judgement, decision making.
- **People competencies**: typically about teams, collaboration, empathy, interpersonal skills, influencing, communication, personal development, motivation, coaching.

Here is a typical list of competencies used by an organisation as part of its selection process. The organisation has not clustered them in terms of task, thought, people but, as you can see, it is quite simple to do this:

Planning to achieve results	TASK
Broad-based commercial thinking	THOUGHT
Innovation and change	THOUGHT
Team leadership	PEOPLE
Analytical thinking	THOUGHT
Developing self and others	PEOPLE
Operational implementation	TASK

If you have access to the competencies in advance, you can prepare by doing this clustering yourself. This will pay off during the interview in terms of your ability to quickly identify the focus of the question. Once you have clustered the competencies you can start to think about your best examples and illustrations to get across the relevant attributes.

The table below gives some examples of organisational competencies that we have clustered for you.

Task	Thought	People
Sales focus	Change orientated	Team leadership
Planning and organising	Creativity and innovation	Collaborative working
Commitment to results	Strategic thinking	Engaging others
Energy and drive	Broad-based business thinking	Networking and communicating
Achievement orientated	Provides vision and direction	Emotional intelligence
Commercially driven	Creative problem solving	Empathy / developing rapport
Delivering results	Analytical thinking	Motivating others
Project planning	Thinks outside the box	Building and developing teams
Project management	Exploring new ideas	Influencing and persuading
Resource management	Inventive and imaginative	Team working
Target orientated	Judgement and decision making	Interpersonal skills

Having the model in your head, you can shape your answers more effectively. Holding on to three ideas – task, thought, people – is a lot easier than trying to memorise and then reference a whole competency framework in 'real time'! The model lets you quickly identify that 'this is a *task* question' and pinpoint the key aspects of your style that you want to put across in your answer.

Take the following example:

'Can you tell us about a time when you had to plan something in detail; how did you go about it?'

This is a 'task' question; it is about operational delivery and the competency being explored is 'planning to achieve results', so your answer should play to this expectation, as follows:

"*OK, well a recent example is my coordination of the Birmingham exhibition: when I'm planning I like to make sure that all factors are considered, so I drew up a detailed checklist which I then turned into a project plan. It contained all the key dependencies and resources mapped against the time line. The deadline was quite tight so I did daily checking to make sure that the exhibition design team, the sales team and the venue team were all talking to each other and that they were all operating to the same plan.*"

The emphasis in the answer is on the implementation steps taken – the *tasks* that were performed (I considered all factors; I drew up a checklist; I turned it into a project plan; I checked daily) – so that the questioner is reassured about your approach to planning.

Holding on to three ideas – task, thought, people – is a lot easier than trying to memorise and then reference a whole competency framework in 'real time'!

Suppose that you had given the following answer to the same question, this time giving a people-based answer:

"*OK, well a recent example is my coordination of the Birmingham exhibition: when I'm planning I like to get the team together early, so we had a number of meetings where we agreed who was doing what. Everyone enjoys this process; it gets the creative juices flowing and it gives everyone a chance to contribute early on; I also made sure that I got the right people on the team with representatives from design, sales and from the venue. That way everyone knew what everyone else was doing.*"

On the face of it, this is not a particularly poor answer, but it does not fit the model that the interviewer has in his/her head; this makes it more difficult for them to quickly identify you as someone who knows how to go about detailed planning. Your answer tells them that you give emphasis to collaborative, team-based work, that you are interested in whether people are enjoying their work and that you see the importance of communication; but that is not what they were exploring in their 'task' question. At the very least this means that they will have to refocus you and ask follow-up questions – if they are good at their job. If they are not, you will simply have missed the chance to tick this particular box.

Researching the interview situation

Nervousness is an inevitable part of interviews for most of us, and anything we can do to minimise it is likely to be helpful. Once again, the more you can find out in advance about the actual interview situation, the better. If you can, you should at least find out the following:

- The timing of the interview: how long will it last? This will give you a sense of how expansive you can afford to be with your answers.
- The interview format: will it be a structured, competency-based interview? What, if any, other components will there be to the interview, for example, a biographical interview or an element based on your CV and work history?
- Who will be interviewing you: will it be one person or a panel of two or more?
- Details of venue: the last thing you need is to be in a panic about finding the right location!

A lot of this information should be contained in your invitation to the interview, but don't hesitate to contact the organisation to clarify any of the above points about which you are not clear.

Dealing with more than one interviewer

Most structured, competency-based interviews will take at least one hour and it is common for them to be conducted by two people so that they can share the job of taking notes. Knowing this in advance can help you to visualise the interview situation and minimise any apprehension you may feel. There are some points to bear in mind if you are going to be interviewed by more than one person.

■ While your attention should be mainly directed to the person who has asked you the question (about 70%), you should take time to 'include' the whole panel as you answer questions. This can be a matter of simply taking the trouble to make eye contact naturally with the other panel members, or of referring to them as you give your answers. For example 'Yes, I think I am pretty detail conscious – the example I gave Peter earlier was one where I had to be right on top of the detail.'

■ Make sure you don't accidentally ignore anyone, for example because they are sitting at the end of the panel table or because they are quieter.

■ In panel interviews it is common for the interviewers to take one competency area each; this makes it easier for you to identify the topic area under consideration.

Dealing with questions on CVs and work history

It is also quite common, especially for more senior-level jobs, for your CV and work history to be explored in detail – often as a separate part of the interview. You should be ready for this – think through the key points you want to get across in relation to the experience you have described in your application or CV. Make sure, if there are any gaps in your work record, that you have a clear explanation of what you were doing. Trying to gloss over any periods of unemployment or hoping that they will not be noticed is very unwise; if the interviewer thinks you are prevaricating or being less than honest this will colour their whole impression of you. It is much better to explain positively how you used any down time, so think this through in advance.

When the interview contains a biographical or work history element, it is common for the interviewer to ask about high points or low points of any particular experience and what you learned from them. As part of your preparation, go through your CV and ask yourself the same questions about the key experiences you have listed. For example:

- What do I consider were my main successes in that role/situation?
- What helped or hindered me?
- What were the key skills/knowledge I brought to the situation?
- What did I learn?

This is an important aspect of preparation because the interviewer will use your answers to assess things such as your objectivity, your self-awareness, your willingness to self-evaluate and your learning style. These are usually quite hard questions to answer 'off the cuff' because, even for the most quick-witted, they need some reflection time: so do your reflecting in advance. See Chapter 7 for more advice on answering non-competency-based questions.

Researching yourself: assets and risks

The final element of preparation that we will cover here is the time you should give to weighing yourself, your style and your assets/risks in relation to both the interview situation and the job. The details of how to make sure that your assets come across in terms of task, thought and people will be dealt with in detail in Chapters 4, 5 and 6, so here we will focus on other elements of self-awareness that are relevant to you as an interviewee.

Despite having conducted hundreds of interviews, it still surprises us how unaware people often are of their impact during the interview. So, how well do you know yourself? What do your friends/family/colleagues say about your impact when you are not around? Probably the only way you will find out is by asking them!

Your impact at interview

Part of your preparation should include a long, hard look in the mirror (metaphorically speaking), so as to make as objective an assessment as possible of people's likely first impression of you. Here are some questions you can ask of yourself – or of others – to help build self-awareness of your impact.

"How confident do I sound when talking about myself?"

Research shows that interviews often overemphasise – and thus tend to put too much weight on – social confidence and verbal fluency. Good interviewers will try to get beyond this so that they are not overly influenced by the 'spin' a candidate is putting on their achievements. Nevertheless, understanding how confident and fluent you typically sound is important. It's also worth remembering that for most people nervousness has a dampening effect on normal levels of confidence and fluency. Sources you can use to assess this include your friends, feedback from previous interviews and your own knowledge of whether, for example, people typically see you as thoughtful and quiet or expressive and extrovert.

Thinking about yourself objectively can be difficult, which is why you need to give time to this element of your preparation. You may even want to record yourself giving answers to some of the sample questions in this book. There is no substitute for actually 'saying the words out loud' as part of your preparation. How does your voice sound? How quickly do you speak? Do the words you use make you sound confident? (Too many positives risk making you sound arrogant.) Do the words you use make you sound too modest? (Too many negatives will make you appear to be self-doubting and uncertain.) A lot of people find this balance hard to achieve, so do practise out loud.

It is worth visualising the interview situation, as a way of mentally preparing yourself.

"Are there any mannerisms or verbal 'ticks' I need to be aware of?"

Examples of verbal 'ticks' include 'ums', nervous coughs, nervous laughs, sighs etc. Other mannerisms may include fidgeting, an unusual posture or tooth tapping. Introspection can only take you so far with these; you need feedback from other people who know you well, and you need to ask them to be really honest and objective. Only worry about mannerisms if people tell you that they get in the way. Changing deeply ingrained mannerisms is not easy, and you don't want to end up looking self-consciously 'stiff' or uncomfortable.

If you need to change any of these things, give yourself plenty of time to work at them and practise. People tend to make the best impact at interview when they appear authentic and 'comfortable in their own skins' – so yes, do prepare, but don't change anything that will get in the way of 'you' coming across as a person.

"How formal or how open and friendly do I appear – particularly in the pressure of an interview situation?"

It is surprising how easy it is to appear overly stern at interview! It comes from concentration and from listening hard – the result being that we frown and our faces end up being less mobile than normal. Once again, care is needed in trying to modify this kind of behaviour – after all, sitting through an interview with a grin glued to one's face is less than helpful – but it does help to be aware of your 'natural' impact and whether it is likely to be an asset or a potential risk. Once again, this kind of preparation needs to be done well in advance.

Assets and risks in terms of the job

Your research into the competencies needed for the role comes into its own here; again, we would suggest using the 'task, thought, people' model as a way of checking – in broad terms – how your experience, skills, competencies and personal attributes map onto the organisation's requirements. We have already talked about how to use this model during the interview, but it is also worth using it as a way of getting a broad picture of where you are likely to be perceived as relatively strong or weak in terms of their criteria. So ask yourself:

■ Am I likely to come over as a TASK person? Is a lot of my experience about operational delivery; are my best examples about driving things through against deadlines; do I find it easiest to talk about delivery, plans and targets?

■ Am I likely to come over as a THOUGHT person? Is a lot of my experience about developing ideas or strategy; are my best examples about creativity and innovation; do I find it easiest to talk about analysis, judgement and insight?

■ Am I likely to come over as a PEOPLE person? Is a lot of my experience about getting results through others and developing people; are my best examples about communication and engagement; do I find it easiest to talk about influencing, coaching and collaborating?

For most of us, as we have seen, one or two of these areas tend to be more highly developed than the others, often because of our natural preferences or our experience. But it is worth giving some thought to how your natural preferences are likely to come to the fore during the interview. If, for example, your analysis tells you that you are most likely to impress interviewers as a *thought* person, with a strong second preference in terms of *people*, then you can shape your preparation to ensure that you are able to call up examples of detailed implementation, meeting deadlines and delivering against obstacles so as to reinforce your 'task' credentials if required. The risk, otherwise, is that you will find yourself less able to tackle questions based in one or more of these domains.

More guidance on how to develop your answers in each of the three areas of the 'task, thought, people' model is provided in Chapters 4, 5 and 6.

IN A NUTSHELL

Doing some basic homework is essential if you are to show off your many talents to best advantage. Key preparation steps to remember are:

- Research the organisation and/or department; you don't need to be an expert, but you should be able to demonstrate that you are interested in them.
- Find out as much as you can about the selection criteria; knowing what they are likely to be looking for makes it much easier for you to focus your preparation.
- Research the interview process itself: who, how and when.
- Prepare yourself; understand your assets and risks in relation to the job, get yourself in the right frame of mind and work on your personal impact.

3 DURING THE INTERVIEW

Another book in this series, *You're Hired! Interview*, gives a lot of excellent coverage on how best to conduct yourself during an interview, but we felt a short guide here would be useful (we advise you to read the other book if you want more detail). Most of the points are reiterated throughout this book at appropriate points, but this chapter is your one-stop reference on how to present yourself to best advantage during the interview. This chapter will cover:

- the interview situation

- building rapport

- being authentic and credible

- the way you answer questions – how to help the interviewer

- closing the interview.

Arriving for the interview

We are going to assume that you have done your homework about the organisation, the competencies and the specific role you have applied for, and that you also know what the format of the interview will be. We are also assuming that:

- you know where the interview is being held (do a dry run if you can so that you are sure about travel time and location)
- you will arrive with time to spare (give yourself time to relax and catch your breath)
- you are well turned out and set to impress!

All of the above will have an impact on how comfortable you feel, and therefore on how you conduct yourself during the interview.

The interview situation

An interview can feel like a contest, a situation where you are in the dentist's chair and the interviewer is trying to extract information from you or catch you out in some way. The best interviews should not be like this. A better way to think about it is as a meeting where both sides are going to share information and come to a mutual decision about suitability or 'fit' with a particular organisation or role. The more you can think about the interview in these terms, the better able you will be to 'be yourself' and benefit from the guidance that follows in this chapter. Most of what you will read below is focused on removing any barriers between you and the interviewer, thus letting them go away with the feeling that they know the 'real you' – as well as having heard about your many positive attributes!

Professional but 'human' is the ideal impact you should be seeking to achieve.

Building rapport

A well-trained interviewer will be working hard to establish rapport, setting you at your ease so that you can perform at your best, but you too have some responsibilities in this regard. Interviews – and interviewers – will vary in terms of the amount of formality or relaxation that is encouraged, and in the first few minutes of entering the interview room and meeting the person (or people) you should be gauging the tone of the interview. Meeting the expectations of the interviewer – in terms of your behaviour – is an important part of rapport building because it helps to put *them* at ease.

FIRST IMPRESSIONS

In practice, most interview situations are about two strangers meeting each other for the first time. The more you can do to make these first few minutes relaxed, the better. If you look and act tense, it is likely that the interviewer will also feel a degree of tension. At the same time – even though they will work hard to put you at ease – they will form an impression of you that will take some time to shift.

In general, match your behaviour and conversation to that of the interviewer; if they are brisk and businesslike, then be polite and respond accordingly – don't try to have a conversation about the weather or the traffic if they are clearly not interested. At the same time if they – and they often will – ask you about your journey, then respond in kind; ask them how their day is going, how far they have to travel to work and so on. You need to be alert to the fact that the interviewer will need to get down to business at some point, so be guided by them.

Think of an interview as a meeting where both sides share information and come to a mutual decision about 'fit'.

Other ways in which you can make a good impression on the interviewer include:

■ Being sensitive to the fact they need to manage time: be guided by their hints – or indeed instructions – to move the conversation on.

- Showing interest in the questions that are being asked: you can indicate this both verbally and non-verbally, for example by head nodding in response to the relevance of the question or by actually saying that you recognise the merit of the question. Examples include:
  - *"That's a good question"*
  - *"Yes, I think that's a very relevant point"*
  - *"I can see that you're trying to focus in on my planning skills here"*
  - *"That's an interesting question"*

Using these phrases can also buy you precious thinking time!

- Signalling what is going on: for example, if you lose the thread of the point you are making, don't just plough on regardless but say, 'I'm sorry, I've lost the thread here, can you remind me of the original question?' This helps the interviewer to 'manage' you.
- Being alert to the interviewer's tone, while not assuming from the interviewer's demeanour that you can assess the impact you are having or how well you are doing. They have a professional job to do, which often means they will be quite focused. Don't let this put you off. The interviewer will get annoyed if you are continually seeking approval for your answers with phrases like *'was that the right answer?'*, or *'is that OK, you look a bit worried?'*

Things that will definitely get in the way of rapport include:

- Too much questioning of the intent of a question or of the purpose of the process. Phrases like *'why are you asking that question?'* or *'why do you keep asking me for examples?'* will not go down well. It will make you sound suspicious and cagey. It's fine to clarify if you are unsure about a particular question, but don't make it sound as if you are questioning the interviewer's professionalism or motives.
- Too much challenging of the basis of the question, or telling the interviewer what they should be asking. For example, *'I'm not sure that your question is relevant, given my experience'* or *'I think a more relevant question would have been …'* are not likely to help the interviewer warm to you.
- Referring to preparation notes. During the interview itself, it is very hard to maintain rapport if you are trying to read notes. It also looks as if you are trotting out a prepared answer rather than answering in real time. If

you must refer to notes, you need to position their use very carefully, for example by explaining that you just want to make sure you are accurate about numbers, or that you want to make sure you have remembered events in the right order. Our advice would be to avoid using notes if at all possible.

■ Inappropriate use of humour. You need to be very sure of your ground – and your talent in positioning jokes – before you risk throwing in the odd funny story or pun. You cannot know the interviewer's sense of humour and you are as likely to get it wrong as to get it right. An interview is no place to be taking this kind of risk.

Being authentic and credible

The interviewer will be more reassured about your answers, and therefore your capabilities, if they feel they are dealing with the 'real' you. In other words, the more authentic and credible you can be, the better. What does this mean in practice?

■ Try to avoid putting on an act. The more you can let your natural style of interaction come through, the better. The interviewer won't feel that they are having to see behind a mask.

■ Use self-disclosure. Share information about yourself (appropriately!) as a way of demonstrating that you are open and honest. Volunteering information in this way has a powerful impact in terms of authenticity and credibility; not only does it show that you are not trying to hide anything, but it also shows that you have the confidence to recognise some (hopefully minor) flaws. Self-disclosure, when well used, also gives you the chance to demonstrate self-awareness; this always impresses, because if you can show a degree of objectivity about yourself, the interviewer is likely to get the impression that you can apply this same skill more broadly in their business.

■ Build trust. Even the most affable interviewer is constantly monitoring how much trust they can have in your answers, how much you are exaggerating your attributes, how honest you are being. Once you lose trust it is almost impossible to win it back in the short time you have available, so don't put it at risk! Don't lay claim to experience that you don't have, and don't pretend to have knowledge that you don't have. Remember that the interviewer doesn't have to catch you out in an untruth – all they have to do is be unsure – for it to have an impact on their assessment of you – and not for the better.

■ Be interesting. As part of your preparation you will have recalled some relevant examples of your experience to illustrate your capabilities. Some of us are much more factual in our ways of describing things, while others tend to be more colourful, painting a picture of what happened. Clearly there is a balance to be found here, but it is worth going over your examples and 'stories' to assess their interest level. If necessary, think of ways to add richness (while sticking to the truth) to the story, people, places, events that make your description more vivid (but not more long-winded!).

■ Be interested. All interviewers will be concerned to assess your motivation to come and work in their organisation. You need to signal your interest, both in response to specific questions and when you get the chance to ask some of your own at the end of the interview (see next page).

■ Protect your credibility. In Chapter 2 we suggested that as part of your preparation you should 'take a look at yourself in the mirror' to see if you need to be aware of any quirks or mannerisms that are likely to affect an interview situation. The same holds true for what you say. If you have led an outrageous and bohemian youth, then you may want to consider what effect sharing information about it will have on the interviewer. Remember that they will have very little other information about you to go on – you don't want to scare them with stories about your riotous behaviour when they have no context for interpreting it! In the same way, you should mention unusual hobbies or pastimes carefully. Highly colourful examples will stick in the interviewer's mind, so be sure that they are the images you want them to have.

The interviewer will be more reassured about your answers, and therefore your capabilities, if they feel they are dealing with the 'real' you.

LASTING IMPRESSIONS

At a practice interview session we staged some years ago, the young woman being interviewed was asked 'What do you do in your spare time?' She answered – with great enthusiasm – 'I breed rats'. With the years that have passed we doubt that the interview panel can remember anything of the woman in question – but we bet they remember that she bred rats!

The way you answer questions

In the coming chapters we provide a lot of guidance and examples of the best ways of answering questions, but it is worth making some general points here. A good interviewer will give you a lot of guidance about their expectations – particularly in the context of a competency-based interview, where they will have a clear structure that they want to follow.

From your point of view, you are likely to leave the best impression if you are focused, professional but conversational in your style of answering. You will get a lot of guidance on this later, but here are some specific 'dos' and 'don'ts'.

DO

- Listen carefully to the questions you are asked. As well as noting whether the interviewer is expecting an answer about task, thought or people, you should pay particular attention to phrases like 'can you give me an example?' This means that the interviewer wants you to describe something that really happened.
- Make it clear what your role was in any situation you are describing. Try to find a balance between using inclusive terms like 'we' did something (shows team orientation and modesty) and 'I' did something (shows much more clearly what your personal role was). Overuse of 'we' will leave the interviewer unsure about your personal involvement.
- Avoid using too much jargon in your answers. Don't assume that the interviewer will be impressed – or indeed will know what you are talking about – if you pepper your answers with too many technical terms or business acronyms.

- Aim to be thorough but concise in the answers you give. Interviewers' hearts tend to sink when they hear phrases like *'OK I need to give you some background first'*, followed by a 10-minute description of the history of ABC Ltd. Aim to produce answers that are no more than 2 minutes in length – as you practise this you will realise that 2 minutes is quite a long time to keep talking. (Two minutes is about the time it would take you to read a closely typed A4 page out loud.) If the interviewer wants more information, they will ask for it.
- Be aware of the speed at which you talk. It is hard to monitor this in 'real time' during the interview, so it needs to be part of your preparation. Get some feedback, or listen to a recording of yourself. Talking too quickly when under pressure and when the adrenalin is flowing is a common fault which needs to be remedied before the interview.

DON'T

- Be long winded. Try to assess in the early stages of the interview how much detail the interviewer is after. Are they interrupting you and trying to move you on, or are they pausing and asking you to 'say a bit more'. Be alert to this and try to modify your answers accordingly.
- Be too terse. If you are asked a specific 'closed' question such as 'how many people were in your team at that point?', then a short answer is fine, but most of the interviewer's questions will be 'open', asking you to describe or explain something, and one-sentence answers to these questions will make it hard work for the interviewer.
- Focus on negatives during your answers. 'Difficult' situations tend to stick in our minds and are often easier to recall. While they will show that you can overcome obstacles and persevere, too many will start to make your working life sound like a horror story! This is why we recommend recalling examples of things you have done well, projects that had a good result, as part of your preparation.

Closing the interview

Research shows that what we say in the first 2 minutes of meeting someone and what we say in the last 2 minutes have a disproportionate effect on the impression we give. For this reason it is well worth thinking about what your closing remarks will be.

At the end of the interview you will nearly always be asked if you have any questions you would like to ask. It is worth giving this exchange some thought. You should be aiming to ask a question – or a couple of questions – that show you are thoughtful about and interested in the role or the organisation. This is not the time to produce a list of ten detailed queries about aspects of the job. The interviewer will usually be trying to manage time, so it is worth assessing whether they have allowed 5 minutes, or 15 minutes, for this closing stage of the discussion. At the same time, asking no questions risks sounding as though you are not really interested and motivated to join them.

It sounds obvious, but the best questions to ask are ones that you genuinely want to know the answer to – they will sound authentic and relevant. It is certainly OK to ask questions about 'next steps', or when the organisation is planning to make a decision about the appointment; it is also quite appropriate to ask questions of a more general kind, such as *'Do you know the size of the new team yet?'* or *'When is the move to the new site planned?'* or *'How are customers responding to the new branding?'*

Avoid questions that sound too 'needy', such as *'Are you interviewing a lot of people for this job?'* or that are naive and should have been answered by your preparation, for example *'So how many stores do you have?'* or *'Are you based here in Leeds?'* or *'Do you have a manufacturing and a sales department?'* You should really know the answers to these questions in advance, and asking them at the end of the interview risks sounding as though you haven't done your homework or are not really interested in their business.

The parting shot

How you close the conversation is nearly as important as how you start it. It is your final chance to leave a good impression in the mind of the interviewer. Here are some final tips:

■ Leave on a positive note. Signal that you have found the conversation really interesting or very informative, or that you have really valued the chance to learn a bit more about the business.
■ Encourage continued contact. Depending on the nature of the interview,

it may be appropriate for you to ask if there is any more information they need, to check that they have your contact details or to ask if it would be appropriate for you to seek some general feedback on the interview at some future date. Asking for feedback in this way is a final signal that you are developmentally orientated and keen to build your self-awareness.

■ Leave purposefully. Don't bolt from the room, but don't shuffle out either!

IN A NUTSHELL

Manage the impression you make by avoiding barriers that may get in the way of establishing a positive relationship with the interviewer, and by knowing the signals that will create a good impression. In summary:

■ Think about and work to build rapport with the interviewer.
■ Be yourself as much as you can: the more authentic you are, the less the interviewer will feel that they have to 'get behind the mask'.
■ Manage the way you answer questions: professional, human, not too terse, not too long-winded.
■ Close the interview positively – leave a good last impression.

4 TASK-BASED QUESTIONS

Example Interview Answers

How you get things done is an obvious area of interest for a prospective employer and task-based questions aim to get at just this. The 'task' arena is about how you organise yourself and others to deliver; how you coordinate people and resources to achieve something; how you structure, implement and execute projects/ assignments in order to achieve objectives. In this chapter we will:

■ show you how to recognise task-based questions

■ show you how to prepare

■ give you examples of questions and of poor and better answers.

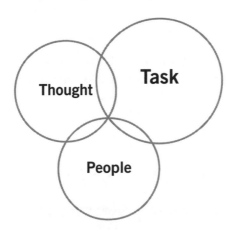

Putting the **CAR** model to work

In Chapter 2 we showed how the 'task, thought, people' model can be used to prepare yourself for interview; now is the time to put this preparation to work. This section looks at how to recognise questions that are trying to get at your 'task' skills and competencies, as well as showing you a range of questions and answers. The example questions and answers will be pitched at different levels and we will go through to identify the main 'dos' and 'don'ts' of framing strong answers to these tough questions.

THE **CAR** MODEL

Remember the **CAR** model from Chapter 1? The acronym will help you to structure answers in a way that gives the interviewer a clear picture of what you did in a particular situation. It stands for:

- **C**ircumstances (or Context)
- **A**ction (what you did)
- **R**esults (what happened as a result of what you did).

We will use this model to critique the answers to all the example questions that follow.

Recognising task-based questions

What should you quickly look out for in an interview question to tell you that the interviewer is looking for a task-based answer? From our experience, questions containing a combination of the following words should trigger your recognition of a task focused question. Words like:

organise	goal	objective	delivery	targets	deadlines
budget	system	process	steps	stages	project
manage	implement	execution	monitoring	controlling	measure

Questions containing words or phrases built around these 'task' words are likely to require a clear, structured answer from you, showing what you actually did.

Task-based questions are trying to reveal your approach to getting things done. Are you methodical and systematic in your delivery style – or are you a more creative implementer? How do you go about prioritising or project management? How do you track and monitor progress to ensure delivery to target, budget or quality standards?

More than for other kinds of questioning, it is important that the medium and the message line up in the way that you build your answers. In other words, if your answers are poorly structured and all over the place, it will be hard to convince the interviewer that you are systematic and organised in the way that you implement tasks!

Task-based questions are trying to reveal your approach to getting things done.

Preparing to respond to task-based questions

We are not suggesting that you should memorise answers in advance of an interview – you should always frame your answers based on the question you are actually asked. However, it does help to have in your mind some good examples of pieces of work you have delivered – or have been closely involved with – that showcase your delivery and 'task' competencies. It can be surprisingly difficult to come up with your best examples in the heat of the interview moment.

Have in mind some good examples of work you have delivered that showcases your delivery and 'task' competencies.

PRACTISE USING *CAR*

Spend a few minutes considering the following. Try to recall examples of situations where you have had to:

- organise something relatively complex
- deliver something to a tough deadline
- implement a new process or system
- overcome significant obstacles to achieving an objective
- coordinate resources to achieve a goal.

Use the **CAR** process to frame a short description of each example, making sure that you cover the **circumstances**, the **action** you took and the **result**.

EXAMPLE INTERVIEW ANSWERS

The remainder of this chapter contains example interview questions and answers to give you a feel for how to interpret and respond in the best way. We will help you to explore what not to say, by reviewing poor answers, and will show you better answers on which you can model your own responses.

Levels of question

We have split our examples into three broad sections to differentiate between different levels of role:

- Graduate/trainee management
- Middle management
- Senior management.

At entry and middle levels of recruitment, the task domain is mostly about self-organisation, planning and personal delivery style and how you meet deadlines and quality standards; at more senior levels it is about mustering resources and lining them up to deliver the required goal.

We suggest that you use the examples from all levels as part of your practice: the intent of the question will be relevant, only the expected scope of the answer will change.

Graduate/trainee management level

At graduate level it is all the more important to have thought through the examples you are planning to use – most obviously because you may not have a wealth of work-based examples that you can call on. Interviewers will be realistic in their expectation in this regard, so don't be put off. It will help, however, if you can make your examples as concrete as possible and, ideally, related to something that they, in turn, can relate to the job. For instance, using an example of how you planned your work study and revision would not be as strong as using an example of how you planned a meeting or an event.

Remember what the interviewer is looking for; they want to see signs that you can organise yourself to deliver, that you think through the steps and stages needed to accomplish something, that you met deadlines and/or achieved a successful result. If you only have limited work experience to call on, try to choose examples that involve some or all of these elements. Examples that we have seen used successfully include:

- the organisation of a visit or field trip
- contributing to running a one day conference
- plans or processes you have used to ensure that you met a deadline
- planning and organising a holiday
- your approach to delivering results in a part time or vacation job.

Here come the examples.

Interviewer: Can you tell me about a situation where you had to organise something in detail?

 Poor answer:

"Yes, well, when I was working in the supermarket over Christmas I redid the Saturday work roster because so many people were off sick; I had a chat with all the Saturday team and we agreed that something had to be done because we were all working too much overtime. It had got to the point that one more person going sick would have meant that we were seriously understaffed, we wouldn't be able to restock shelves or even fully staff all the tills."

Why is this a poor response?

Mainly because the interviewer is going to have to ask a lot of follow-up questions to find out what actually went on. The circumstances have been partially described, but not in enough detail; the action taken is very woolly – 'I had a chat with the team' – and the outcome or result is not covered at all. The clue is in the question: the interviewer wants to know how you organise, so explain the process that you went through.

✓ Better answer:

"*Yes, well, when I was working in the supermarket at Christmas we had a staffing problem because so many people were off sick. I took on the job of redoing the work roster because it was clear that we were going to be understaffed if nothing was done. I checked availability with all the existing staff, matched this with the staffing requirement and then built in an allowance for temps in case anyone else should fall sick. I showed the new roster to the team and got them to agree where they were willing to put in extra hours. Everyone was very cooperative and the end result was that we kept to full staffing for the whole period.*"

This is still a relatively short answer, but it does cover the **CAR** format:

- **Circumstances** are covered: 'it was Christmas and we had a staffing problem'.
- **Action** is explained: 'I checked availability and matched it with the staff requirement'.
- **Result** is described: 'we kept to full staffing for the whole period'.

This answer is likely to tell the interviewer that you are purposeful and structured in tackling this kind of challenge.

Can you think of any ways in which this answer could have been still stronger? Here are some suggestions:

- A little more detail would have made the answer richer, for example, how many staff were involved, how big was the shortfall, how did you identify the problem?

- Make your own role clear: 'I took on the job' does not make it clear whether you were being proactive or were responding to someone else's request.
- Timing: over what period did this all happen – hours, days? Putting in some of this detail makes the example more vivid and convincing.

Interviewer: Tell me about your experience of managing or monitoring expenditure against a budget – give me an example if you can.

 Poor answer:

"*Well, when I was secretary of the sports and leisure committee I was responsible for looking after the amenities budget – basically the budget for any minor repairs or refurbishments that were needed to the sports hall and changing facilities. It was really a matter of checking that we could afford any proposed repairs, that we got the cheapest quote and that the trades people got paid at the end of the work.*"

Why is this a poor response?

As well as missing out the **C A R** structure, the example described does not give the interviewer any clear evidence about your approach to monitoring and controlling and this is probably what they are after. The intent behind this task based question is likely to be as follows:

- Can this person control things?
- Does this person monitor what is going on so that they can control things?
- How does this person monitor what is going on so that they can control things?
- Does this person measure and check the right things to ensure that the flow (be it money, time, electricity or project days) is predictable and that the resource won't run out unexpectedly?

The answer above does not cover any of these points.

✓ Better answer:

"Well, when I was secretary of the sports and leisure committee I was responsible for looking after the amenities budget – basically the budget for any minor repairs or refurbishments that were needed to the sports hall and changing facilities. At the start of the year I asked all the committee members for their predictions for expenditure and for their spending priorities. I matched these to the budget and then made an allowance for unexpected repair bills – the previous secretary told me that about 20% of the budget was a sensible contingency fund. I then made a prediction for our quarterly spend so that I could keep tabs on the budget throughout the year. In fact we had very few unexpected repairs that year so we finished with a small surplus."

Here the **CAR** format is much more clearly followed:

- Circumstance – managing the budget for minor repairs
- Action – predicting spend, checking spend
- Result – a small budget surplus showing that the spend had been effectively controlled

At the same time this answer shows that a systematic approach has been taken to measuring, monitoring and thus controlling the relevant resource – in this case money. The interviewer will be reassured that this person is diligent in ensuring that they have the right processes and the right information to manage (or control) the outcome.

Interviewer: Can you give me an example of a time when you had to deliver something to a tight deadline?

 Poor answer:

"In my first job I had a role in a small marketing department. We were under a lot of pressure because of three exhibitions that were coming up over the next 3 months. We decided that we had to make some decisions in terms of priorities otherwise we would risk failing to have all the stands ready in time. The key to hitting the deadlines was recognising that we had to outsource some of the design work so that we could concentrate on the Excom exhibition, which was by far the most important. I was never convinced that the other two

exhibitions were relevant to us at all – in fact I think we should have pulled them – and I'd have been really unhappy about putting Excom at risk so I think it was the right decision."

This is a task-based question; the key terms are 'deliver' and 'tight deadline'. The answer above does not give a convincing picture in these terms. All we discover from this answer is that 'some decisions were made about priorities' and that 'some work was outsourced'; we can't be sure about this person's role in the process because of the use of 'we'. The rest of the answer focuses on negative aspects and tells us nothing about the result. The upshot is that the interviewer has not learned much about this person's approach to delivering under pressure, which is the purpose of the question.

 Better answer:

"We were under a lot of pressure in marketing because we had to prepare for three exhibitions all with tight deadlines. The exhibitions were all in mid-May and we were already in April. The lead time was five weeks, which is very tight to get all the design work done and I could see we had a problem. I decided to prioritise the Excom work and to outsource the design of the other two exhibitions, which were less critical in terms of our marketing plan. I made it clear to the team that the Excom material had to be ready for proofing in 3 weeks and I built a daily checklist to make sure we were on target. I used the same approach with the outsourced design, getting daily updates from the design agencies to track progress and to make sure there would be no surprises in terms of the costs. In the end we hit the target for all three exhibitions and I was very happy with the design quality we achieved."

Hopefully you can see why this is better. Think of **CAR** again:

■ **Circumstances**: the nature and timing of the deadline are explained.
■ **Action**: we now know what was done, how progress was monitored and what objectives were imposed.
■ **Result**: we have a clear statement that the deadline was met to the right quality standards.

More broadly, the interviewee has understood what the interviewer is looking for, namely, a description of what was done to meet a difficult target. From this the interviewer can reasonably surmise that this person is willing to take action – and knows what action to take – in order to deliver an objective. Notice as well that the interviewee has used language that is appropriate to the question area: terms like 'lead time', 'prioritise', 'critical', 'checklist', 'target', 'updates' and 'track progress' all help to show that you understand what the question is getting at.

There is one additional step you can take to impress, and that is *framing* your answer to show that you have understood the questioner's intent and that you have a systematic approach to this kind of situation.

Starting your answer:

"*I try to take broadly the same approach to delivering against tough deadlines; what I usually do is work back from the delivery date, build in some margin for error and then schedule accordingly. For example, we were under a lot of pressure in marketing ...*"

Closing your answer:

"*... and I was very happy with the design quality we achieved. This is pretty much the approach I take when I'm faced with challenging deadlines.*"

It is important not to dwell on your broad approach for too long – remember that the interviewer wants to know what you actually did – but some 'topping and tailing' of your answer, as in the example above, helps the interviewer to be confident that your general approach to this kind of challenge is also consistent and systematic.

Dealing with follow-up questions

Structured interviews involve follow-up and probe questions, so let's take this example one stage further.

For task-based questions, try to give your answers using 'tasky' language. For example, use terms:

- prioritise
- checklist
- plans
- targets
- measures/metrics
- schedule

Interviewer: I see, so what were the main obstacles you had to overcome?

✗ Poor answer:

"Well a lot of stuff got in the way really. The team wanted to try and do all three exhibitions in-house and a lot of time was wasted convincing them that we had to outsource, but I managed this in the end. Once it was clear that I couldn't win the argument to pull the other exhibitions, I concentrated on convincing them that Excom was the important one and that we had to work flat out on it. Another problem was the design agencies. We hadn't used either agency before and I was really worried that they wouldn't be up to our quality standards, especially given the timescale, so I had to spend a lot of time with them getting them up to speed; I was on their backs a lot but it paid off in the end."

This answer manages to be both vague and very negative in its tone: sounding negative is a risk when you are asked to describe 'obstacles' or problems that occurred. What is needed is a much more structured and positively oriented answer, as we show next.

 Better answer:

"There were three main challenges in this situation. First was putting all the evidence in front of the team to make it clear that we had to outsource; once I showed them the work schedule and the key dates they agreed that we had to go to an agency. Second was the challenge of getting the agencies up to

*speed; I got them to come in for a briefing, meeting our team and setting up the review meetings so that we could check progress. Third, I wanted to make sure that we avoided the same situation in the future, so I set up a working group to make sure that we had better scheduling in place to anticipate workflow problems like this.***"**

This follow-up answer is structured, it is clear in describing the steps that were taken and it emphasises positive aspects of the situation, rather than dwelling on negatives. In this case the interviewee has also taken the opportunity to show that they have learned from the experience and done something about it.

WHAT DID YOU LEARN?

Interviewers will often ask 'what did you learn from the situation?' Anticipating this question in your answer is a good way of helping the interviewer out, and it always impresses.

Middle management level

At this level you can anticipate that the questioner will be probing still more and be expecting you to be more 'managerial' in your answers – in other words, to consider the wider consequences of your actions and multiple factors/resources that had to be organised to deliver the result.

Here are some examples.

Interviewer: One of the competencies we are interested in is monitoring and controlling; can you give me an example of a situation where your approach to monitoring was important to achieving an objective?

 Poor answer:

"*Yes, I think that in operational situations such as the one you have here in the dispatch department it's really important that you have a good feel for how everything is running. I use the PRIME 2 system; I think it does a really good job of monitoring batch delivery. If you set it up right you can get instant progress reports, for example relating to particular consignments or to any delays in the system. I relied on it a lot in my last job because it took a lot of the guesswork out of work scheduling. So my approach is to make sure that there is a reliable system in place and I think PRIME 2 is hard to beat.*"

There is not much evidence of **CAR** being applied here. While the answer might be OK as an advert for PRIME 2 (whatever that is!), it doesn't give the interviewer much information about this person's approach to monitoring and controlling. In particular, it fails to give the required concrete example. The mistake here is to 'hear' the last part of the question, 'your approach to monitoring', but to miss the all-important 'give me an example'.

✔ Better answer:

"*Yes, I think the key part of having the right controls is understanding the pressure points in the system and making sure that the monitoring system lets you anticipate problems. Let me use an example from my last job; we had a dispatch department that was consistently overloaded because of unpredictable production. They would be quiet for several hours, then working like crazy because production had released several batches at the same time. I got the dispatch supervisors to monitor throughput for a month to see if there was any way of predicting the workflow, and sure enough there was. I then implemented a system where dispatch could monitor orders coming in; I worked out that the lead time for particular products was predictable. In the short term this was more work for the supervisors – using the order book to predict workload 2 weeks in advance – but in the longer term it smoothed out the peaks and troughs and made everyone's life easier. It also meant that dispatch was much more efficient and that customers got their orders on average a whole day earlier.*"

While there is scope for adding more detail to this answer, it does follow the **CAR** principles.

- **Circumstances:** 'we had a dispatch department that was consistently overloaded'.
- **Action:** 'I implemented a system where dispatch could monitor orders coming in'.
- **Result:** 'dispatch was much more efficient'.

The interviewer can tell what the issue was, what the person did and what the result was. Overall, the answer gives the interviewer relevant information to assess whether this person understands the competency 'monitoring and controlling'.

Interviewer: Can you give me an example of a time when you had to overcome significant obstacles in order to achieve a result or deliver something?

✗ Poor answer:

"*I suppose the best example I can think of is when we had to merge the Bradford and Leeds offices. We had about 30 people in each office – I was managing Leeds – and I was asked to bring the Leeds people over and combine the two sales departments. As you can imagine, there was a lot of resistance but I persevered and managed to get it all done within 3 months. People don't like change so it was never going to be easy; the main thing is to be crystal clear right from the start so people know what to expect. I spent a week in the Bradford office explaining the situation – there was a lot of resistance, especially from the sales managers but some straight talking drove the change through in the end.*"

What's wrong with this answer?

You have probably noted that the basics of **CAR** are present but there just isn't enough information about the obstacles or what was done to overcome them. There are also some sweeping generalisations in the answer – 'people don't like change' – and these are best avoided, since they may contradict the organisation's competencies or the interviewer's preferences!

Let's follow this question through with some probes.

Interviewer: So what were the key obstacles?

✗ Poor answer:

"*Well it was the fact that the sales managers didn't want to change their territories, they were very possessive about them.*"

Interviewer: So what did you actually do?

 Poor answer:

"I talked to them and I compromised; a bit of shuffling of territories meant that they ended up with about the same revenue potential as they had had before."

This is starting to feel a bit like getting blood from a stone. Remember that this is a task-based question; the interviewer wants to know the person's approach to overcoming obstacles. The answers so far do not suggest a systematic approach to meeting these challenges; for example, 'a bit of shuffling of territories' sounds far too offhand. Now this may just be the interviewee's shorthand for a rigorous process of analysis and reallocation, but you can't tell that from the answer. Think what the interviewer is looking for in asking this question – it probably includes:

- *Does this person persist when the going gets tough?*
- *Can this person use alternative methods if plan A is not working?*
- *Does this person have a structured approach to implementation?*
- *Did the person have a clear objective in mind?*
- *How did they ensure that things were happening to time and to budget?*

None of these is adequately dealt with in the answers so far, and the interviewer is going to have to do a lot more probing to get to the facts. The answers below come much closer to dealing with the question well.

✓ Better answer:

"I suppose the best example I can think of is when we had to merge the Bradford and Leeds offices. We had about 30 people in each office – I was managing Leeds – and I was asked to bring the Leeds people over and combine the two sales departments. The first thing I did was set a 'go live' date by which the merger had to be completed. I set out a time line – 2 months – and developed a project plan so that nothing would be missed – there was a surprising amount of detail to consider, everything from terminating leases to transferring customer contact numbers. The second thing I did was to spend a week in the Bradford office to clearly communicate the change and its implications. I had one-to-one meetings with all the sales managers, explaining

the situation and asking them to buy into the plan. There was a lot of resistance initially; they were worried about the implications for their bonuses if their territories changed too much. So, plan B was to sit them all down and agree how territories would be shared. The third step was to create a transition team and to allocate all the tasks from the project plan so that everyone knew who was responsible for what. The result was that everything got done on time and we were all co-located in the Leeds office by the start of May."

Interviewer: So what were the key obstacles?

 Better answer:

"Apart from winning the sales managers over, the biggest challenge was the sheer amount of detail involved. Everything from telephone numbers to getting the sales reps' cards reprinted; strong project management was essential to keeping track of it all. The scariest moment was when it looked as if the lease on the extension to the Leeds office would not come through in time. I had to call a special meeting with our contracts people to make the seriousness of the situation clear – I wasn't prepared to accept any delay in the merger – and, in fairness, they pulled out all the stops and got the contracts signed."

Look back at the list of interviewer's objectives we gave at the end of the 'poor answer' section above. These answers cover all the relevant ground and would leave the interviewer pretty clear about the interviewee's style of delivering this kind of task. Key things to note are:

- the answer itself is structured – 'firstly', 'secondly', etc.
- the question asks about obstacles; a specific obstacle is described, together with how it was overcome
- timescales and objectives are described
- there is sufficient detail that you can tell what the person actually did.

Senior management level

At more senior levels of recruitment you can expect the scope of the questions to be wide, with the interviewer looking for answers that are pitched at the right level. For example, if the job you are applying for is head of training in a large, multi-site organisation, the interviewer is going to want to be reassured that you recognise the scope of the job and that your competencies are up to it. This means that you should try to use examples that reflect the challenges the job will hold. You are unlikely to impress if you limit yourself to examples based on running a small training department in one location. You will need to think of those things that you have been involved in that show you can deliver companywide.

At more senior levels, the interviewer will also be expecting to see that you can deliver through other people, and not just through your own task focus. At department or functional head level (or higher) the interviewer will want to know things like:

- whether you can win and coordinate resources
- the scale of your objective setting
- that you measure and monitor the right things
- that you can create the conditions that let people deliver
- that you are able to initiate, to make things happen.

Interviewer: Quality is a key issue for us at the moment; can you give me an example of a significant quality issue you have had to deal with and tell me how you went about it?

 Poor answer:

"*I've always felt that quality has to be at the heart of business culture, my personal approach is to try and set an example, getting things right first time and avoiding doing the same job twice. I don't think anyone sets out to do a bad job but sometimes management doesn't set the right example. There was a time when I was with ABC Ltd, when customer service levels had dropped off to an unacceptable level. It was a staff turnover issue so I got our recruitment people to change the agencies we were using so as to get a better level of applicant. It didn't happen overnight, but the better-quality staff has started to drive the complaints levels down. I think quality is all about people taking personal responsibility for their actions, it's hard to control quality, you have to build it in.*"

This is a limited answer, too brief on the detail, preceded and followed by a lot of waffle. No sign of **CAR** here. Depending on the seniority of the job, this example might also be too local.

 Better answer:

"*To my mind, quality is often a matter of training people well and letting them know what is needed from them. When I was General Manager at ABC Ltd our customer research began to show that customer satisfaction had started to fall. Now, there are lots of potential reasons for this and I wanted to know in more detail what was going wrong. I brought in some customer service specialists to look at the issue across all our call centres, because if it was affecting one region, chances were it would be affecting the others. The research showed that the main issue was staff turnover; because of the need to get frontline call handlers working quickly we had cut back on the training time and this was showing in terms of how effectively customers were being dealt with – waiting times were too long. I asked the call centre managers to come up with a solution – quickly! I told them that we needed to get the satisfaction figures heading in the right direction in weeks, not months!*"

Interviewer: So what was the outcome?

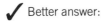 Better answer:

"*Their first reaction was to ask for a bigger training budget, but finances just didn't allow this so I asked them to think again. The eventual solution was to improve the recruitment process – we changed to a recruitment agency rather than doing it in-house and this actually ended up saving us money. Better recruits and a better system for supervising them in the first 3 months made a significant difference.*"

Interviewer: How much difference?

✓ Better answer:

"*Waiting times are now down to below our competitors' average and the last customer survey showed that we had edged up two full points in terms of customer satisfaction. It was too easy to forget that the call handler was our key contact with the customer, a fall in quality here could affect the whole business; it's too easy to think of it as an administrative activity rather than something that adds real value to the business. My job was to recognise this and get the right people to do something about it.*"

This sequence of Q and A shows a much fuller and wide-reaching approach to quality. The reference is to a companywide issue, there is emphasis on taking action, it is clear what was done and the outcome is clearly described. The interviewee has also taken the opportunity to show business-wide consideration of this issue. The interviewer is likely to be convinced that here is a person who recognises a delivery problem and knows how to take the right action to fix it. At senior level, task focus is usually about *initiating* and not just about personal execution, and this answer demonstrates this well.

Interviewer: The proposed merging of our four divisions down to two represents a significant change; can you give me an example of when you have implemented a major initiative or change programme?

✗ Poor answer:

"*Well I've never done anything on the scale of what you are proposing here, but my first reaction is to focus on communication. People are likely to be unhappy, you always get competitiveness in this kind of situation and I would want to get all the key players together and set some ground rules at the outset. It's likely that some jobs are going to be at risk, so we would need to start consultations early. Incidentally, I noticed that XYZ Ltd are talking about consolidation as well – I know that they are in a different market to you but I think it's interesting that so many of the big players are making similar decisions at about the same time. Where was I? I'd probably want to set up a change team as well, made up of people from all the divisions so that we could avoid any duplication of effort. I had to do something similar at ABC Ltd when two sales teams had to be merged; communication was the key, I made sure that people were talking to each other throughout.*"

Here we have a negative, followed by a lot of hypothetical solutions, followed by an irrelevant digression, followed by a poor example; not likely to impress!

✓ Better answer:

"*Yes, you have a significant challenge on your hands. My experience of this kind of merger is that people are at their best when they are clear about what the intention is rather than working in an atmosphere of rumour and suspicion. At ABC Ltd the Board gave me the role of merger coordinator, the job was to bring the sales teams from all the product lines together into a unified sales function. I gave myself the target of achieving an integrated department within 3 months and I pulled together a team to do this. I appointed a head of communications and a head of coordination. They reported to me weekly in terms of the various work streams that were necessary to bring about the change. I separated the coordination and communication roles because my experience is that conflicts arise if the same person is trying to implement and time communication as well – I saw this done badly when I was at XYZ Ltd and I learned the lesson!"*

Interviewer: What did you do in practice, how did you see your role?

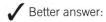 Better answer:

"My job was to keep everyone focused on the target and to provide the support and resources they needed. For example, by working with the two heads I had appointed, the weekly project meetings were a forum where we could anticipate any obstacles and take action to tackle them. There was one point where there was an issue to do with redrafting all the employment contracts to bring them into line. The coordination head pointed this out and I took it on myself to get our legal department to focus on this, bringing them into the project plan and giving them clear timescales for delivering the work. They had their own priorities to worry about, but I made it clear that I wouldn't allow the contracts issue to slow everything down and that other matters they were working on would have to be reprioritised."

Once again, this answer makes the interviewee sound structured, clear about what they did and, just as importantly, attentive to the questioner's need for detail – that's why they asked the follow-up question.

None of the examples given above is perfect, nor are they meant to be 'model answers' that you can paraphrase or memorise. What they do illustrate is the kind of answer that is most likely to impress if you follow the tips we have given.

IN A NUTSHELL

Task-based questions need a structured, task-based answer. The interviewer wants to know what you did and how you did it. To summarise:

- Think through some good, task-based examples of your work in advance.
- Look out for the key words that tell you if the interviewer is expecting a task-based answer.
- Follow the **CAR** structure as you give your answer – **Circumstances, Action, Result**.
- It's OK to top and tail your answers with more general points, but not at the expense of a clear, concrete example.
- Structure your answer, tell the interviewer what you did first, second, third.
- Be succinct and avoid too many digressions or side issues.

5 THOUGHT-BASED QUESTIONS

Example Interview Answers

This chapter focuses on questions that are trying to get at your thinking style; how you plan, prioritise, innovate and consider the bigger picture. As before, it gives you a chance to understand and practise this kind of question, and it is vital reading in preparing for a competency-based interview. In it we:

■ define the competency domain of thought leadership

■ explain how it relates to all roles, irrespective of the level of the role you are applying for

■ give you example interview questions

■ provide example responses.

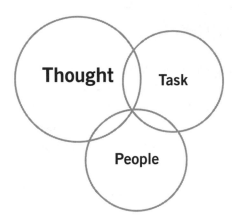

Thought-based questions

There are not many roles that don't require an element of thought leadership. Even the most basic administrative role will require the ability to explore and analyse a problem, identify potential solutions and then implement them. Where solutions do not exist, then creative responses and new ideas are required. Some of the best administrators that we have worked with are those who have been able to discuss with us what we wanted to achieve and then find a way of implementing it by generating new ideas.

For more senior or complex roles, the dimension of thought leadership is about more complex problem solving, involving many variables, longer-term thinking and scenario building, right up to visioning and strategy.

It's an important aspect of most jobs, then, and in this chapter we'll explore how to recognise a 'thought leadership' question, and we'll give you some example questions and answers for different levels of role.

Recognising a 'thought-based' interview question

What are the key ingredients of a 'thought-based' question? What will alert you that the interview is trying to explore aspects of your thinking and problem-solving style? As a rule of thumb, the words below are likely (but not always), to relate to thought leadership, and should therefore trigger your thinking about aspects of your previous roles where you have had to problem-solve in some capacity.

creative	problem	new	strategy
develop	identify	come up with	complex
plan	opportunity	analyse	idea

Another way to recognise a 'thought-based' question is when it does not obviously relate to delivering a task or to interacting with other people; this can be quite hard to spot and sometimes it depends on where the emphasis is in the question. So, for example:

'Tell me about a time where you worked with others to develop a new concept'

is likely to be a 'people' question, rather than a 'thought' question.

Whereas:

'Tell me about a time when you developed a new concept'

is clearly a 'thought' question.

Preparing to respond to thought-based questions

This very simple exercise will help you to prepare and respond to most of the example interview questions that we'll present in this chapter. Where it does not fit directly, there will usually be a way of doing so – finding an angle that makes it relevant to the question being asked.

ACTIVITY 4

GATHERING YOUR THOUGHTS ON THE FOLLOWING:

- an example of where you came up with an idea
- an example of where you had to solve a problem
- an example of where you had to set longer-term direction
- an example of where you had to plan something.

On a sheet of paper just jot down a very broad outline of each issue against the **CAR** model that we introduced in Chapter 1.

If you really struggle to think of examples in one of the four broad areas above, it is likely that it is a potential weakness for you. Equally, it may simply be that you underestimate what you have done to demonstrate competency in that area. One way to address the latter is to speak to a colleague or friend. They may be aware of instances where you have demonstrated this and be able to remind you.

IDENTIFY THE COMPETENCIES TO DEMONSTRATE

As part of your interview preparation you should have identified the organisation's competencies. Once you have these, you can better prepare potential examples to respond to questions.

EXAMPLE INTERVIEW ANSWERS

The remainder of this chapter is given over to example interview questions and answers to give you a feel for how to interpret and respond to the question. It's split into three broad sections to differentiate between different levels of role:

- Graduate/trainee management
- Middle management
- Senior management

Moving up these three levels, responses to questions need to increase in their complexity and level of focus. An easy-to-use general rule is that for a trainee management role the focus is likely to be at the individual level (although not exclusively); at the middle management level, the focus is at team or departmental level; and at senior management level the focus will increasingly be heading towards business unit or even organisational level. Remember, these are generalities and there will always be exceptions, as you will see in some of the examples we provide. When deciding on which level of question to look at, think about the remit of the role rather than exclusively about the level. You may find, for instance, that some of the middle-management level questions will be equally applicable to a more junior role.

Graduate/trainee management level

Interviewer: Please describe a time where you have had to solve a difficult problem.

 Poor answer:

"*Oh yes, there was this time when I had a summer job when there was a clash on the rota. Someone needed to free up a day to enable them to attend a medical appointment, so we needed to sort that out. We looked at the rotas to see who might be able to substitute and obviously needed to take legislation into account to ensure that the shifts were adequately staffed. In the end, someone did 2 hours' overtime to cover for him during his appointment.*"

First of all, this example is very similar to the one provided in Chapter 4 on task-based questions, but it does not adequately differentiate between 'task' and 'thought'. When you use the same or a similar example to respond to two different questions it's important to clearly illustrate how the example relates to the question being asked, and how it differs from your earlier use.

Also, the response lacks structure. Although we know what happened, we don't really know the context, and the credibility is limited. A clearer response would follow **CAR** (Circumstances, Action, Results) and would have given a better insight into the circumstances leading to the situation, the action taken, and the results.

Another problem with this response is that we do not really know what role the interviewee took. What did they contribute to resolving the problem, what data did they draw on, how did they reach a conclusion? Again, the response has limited credibility as a result.

 Better answer:

"*Yes, for a summer job I worked in a place where they operate a shift pattern, with three shifts in a 24-hour period: 7 'till 2, 2 'till 10 and 10 'till 7. I had been asked by the manager to look at the rota for what hours staff were due to be working. One of the other members of staff had requested to be released from*"

a shift as they had an important medical appointment that they needed to attend. The difficulty was that overall, we were slightly short staffed anyway, so finding a way of releasing this person and still being able to adequately staff the shift was going to be difficult. I therefore needed to look at all the information available to me and provide some options for how it might be possible to grant the request.

I looked at the previous 3 weeks' rotas to get a feel for who had done what work; I checked the holiday requests to identify anybody who would definitely not be able to substitute and I looked at what activities had been scheduled which might require a particular staffing level. Finally, I looked at the guidelines which had been laid down for staffing levels in general to ensure that we were complying with legislation. Using all of this information, I generated three possible solutions. The first was to swap two people around, so that one of his off days would fall on the appointment day. The second was to run the shift with just one person fewer – but that meant we were not complying with guidelines. The final option was to ask somebody to cover the 2 hours that he would be away and to pay that person overtime. Even though that was the slightly costlier option, as we would have to pay one person 2 hours' overtime, this was my preferred option. I spoke to the manager and outlined to her the three options I had arrived at and which one I preferred. In the end, she went with my recommendation."

This is a well structured response, in the **CAR** format:

- **Circumstances**: working in a shift system, somebody needed time off for a medical appointment.
- **Action**: exploration of different sources of information, resulting in options being identified and proposed.
- **Result**: decision to offer somebody overtime for a couple of hours, which ensured everybody's needs were met.

The answer provides evidence of what the interviewee actually did – they used 'I' in their response. They also stated what data they looked at and what options they developed from their analysis. All this shows that they have understood the question as a 'thought' question rather than as a 'task' or a 'people' question.

The response could have been better still, there could have been a little more detail on how the decision was actually made, ie how the data was used and what the pros and cons of the options were. For example, the downside of running the shift with just one person less was that not only that it did not comply with the established guidelines, it meant that if there were an emergency this could not be adequately dealt with. The downside of simply swapping people around was that it created problems with childcare arrangements for one person, and so the issue would not have been solved.

Interviewer: Give me an example of a time where you improved something.

 Poor answer:

"As part of my role in the graduate recruitment team, I have responsibility for planning the campaign every year. This was a new responsibility that I had picked up, and I had heard many people complain that the campaigns were not very good. I therefore took it upon myself to improve them. So, I took the plans from last year and made some improvements, such as bringing the whole thing forward by two weeks, changing the booking system as well as the data capture. Overall, the whole thing worked better as a result.

There is not much evidence of CAR here. We do know a little about the circumstance, and we have a very vague outline of the result in that overall the whole thing worked better. What this answer really lacks, though, is a clear explanation of the actions that were taken - we have no sense of the interviewees thinking.*"

 Better answer:

"I was given then responsibility of managing our graduate recruitment campaign. Having heard from line managers in previous years that they did not think the process was as slick as it could be, I decided that as part of managing the process, I would try to introduce some improvements. Specifically, the two key complaints were that the booking system for assessors was "very messy" and that it took us too long to get back to applicants with a decision – this meant that some good candidates were lost as they took offers elsewhere. I therefore focused on improving these two aspects. With regards

to the booking system, I worked with IT to introduce an online booking system. This was interactive, and when line managers logged in to book, it would tell them on which days we still needed assessors, thus making it impossible for some days to be oversubscribed and others to be undersubscribed. From the booking system they could also link directly to the online assessor training materials. With regards to us being late in getting back to applicants, I introduced an online tracking system of candidate performance, in conjunction with one of our suppliers. This enabled us to quickly gather information on candidate performance from across the different locations where we ran assessments and have an overall picture within 30 minutes of the last assessment day finishing. We could therefore make decisions much more quickly. Feedback from the different departments was very positive."

This answer follows the CAR principles far better than the previous response.

- **Circumstances**: There was negative feedback about two specific points.
- **Actions**: The interviewee addressed the two specific points of negative feedback and described the improvements made.
- **Result**: There was positive feedback from the different stakeholder departments.

There is scope to improve the response further still. On the actions front, there could be more detail about the options that were considered and how the interviewee finally decided between the options. On the results front, there could be more specific detail about the benefits as seen by the various stakeholders.

Interviewer: Tell me about a time where you encountered a significant problem with a system, process or procedure. How did you solve it?

 Poor answer:

"*I had felt for a while that our internal resourcing was not very effective. Being a consulting business, how we resourced obviously had implications on the quality of our work and bottom line performance. I therefore suggested that it would be better if one person took on overall responsibility for the resourcing of work. This would mean that one person had the overall, big picture view of how resource was being used.*"

Why is this a poor response? For a start, it is very brief and gives no depth around any aspects of CAR. It has the foundations of a good response, though, as it is clearly about an improvement. Let's look at a better response.

This time we'll give you two possible responses, based on different work scenarios.

 Better answer:

"*I used to work in a resourcing role in a small business where I was responsible for ensuring that our consultants were used in an equitable way. In reality what happened was that when a piece of work came in, project managers would speak to staff directly and allocate work to them. This came to my attention, as consultants would speak to me and complain that they felt work was not being allocated in an equitable way. Our staff survey had also shown a degree of favouritism occurring. So the current system was not working effectively. I made suggestions that all resourcing would need to go through a central person who would take account of availability, skills, performance and so on and discuss with project managers what the resourcing options would be. Rather than me dictating resourcing, it became a joint problem-solving exercise and ensured that project managers were still involved in the process. Feedback so far is that people feel resourcing is now more equitable.*"

The above example demonstrates that a response need not be lengthy – it can be short and punchy. It is also a well structured response around **CAR**.

- **Circumstances**: The respondent worked in a resourcing role in a small business. Feedback about resourcing had not been positive.
- **Actions**: Suggestions were made to resource centrally based on skills, performance and project need.
- **Results**: There was positive feedback and staff survey results were better.

Clearly, there is more information to be gleaned here by an interviewer and there would be follow-up questions to probe about the detail and build confidence, but in essence, the example represents a solid response.

ACTIVITY 5

INTRODUCING CHANGE AND IMPROVEMENT

Think about the situations where you have introduced a change or made an improvement. Write down how what you suggested was different from what you did before. Note down what you based your idea/suggestion on and how you adapted it from what you knew or did previously. This will help you to distil what was different and how you used creative thinking in the workplace. You'll surprise yourself!

Let's look at another two responses to the same question. First a poor one, and then a better one.

✗ Poor answer:

"*My fist training role was as a graduate in a bank. Part of my role required me to report on key financial indicators for the different business units. There was a very tight deadline for this which we never met as we were reliant on information coming in to us from the departments so that we could pull together the report. To get over this, we decided to send out reminder e-mails to all departments to remind them that we needed their input if we were to hit our deadlines. We also offered to support them in pulling the information together so long as they requested our support. Some departments did request support and one of us would see them, spend an hour talking to them to get the important information that we needed to enable us to put the report together.*"

There are several things that are wrong with this response. First of all, the interviewee uses "we" rather than "I". From an interviewer's perspective, they will not know who made the suggestions, or who was actually the driving force behind the improvements. Second, we have no information on the outcomes of this improvement. The response is also not very well structured and therefore difficult to follow. The interviewer's job is as a result, made more difficult so there would likely be many follow up questions.

Here's the second possible response to the question:

 Better answer:

"*Yes, working in the accounts department of the bank, we were responsible for drawing together the monthly management information for various parts of the business. We were a small team of three that were responsible for working on this. The real pressure points were always at was the end of the month when we needed to quickly draw together all financial indicators and report back to the various business units. The problem was that we were reliant on them furnishing us with the raw data that we would then use to prepare our reports. This was not always delivered in a timely fashion, owing to the business pressure that they were under. We were therefore ourselves under pressure to deliver and frequently missed the deadlines, which was clearly not satisfactory. We were unable to put more resource into this, so a solution needed to be found that would enable us to deliver on time. The simple solution would have been to tell them that they just needed to deliver to us in time to enable us to do our job, but the reality was that on, for example, a trading floor, the dealing always took priority over admin-related stuff. What I'd noticed was that part of the problem was the number of different reports that we were having to produce for the different business units which all essentially showed the same information, but just represented differently. The work was therefore repetitive and there was scope for changing this. I suggested that we speak to all BUs about this.*

To support this, I mocked up a report that contained all of the essential information that we provided in the different reports. With this, we were able to have a discussion with the heads of BUs, outlining our difficulties and that if we could agree on a common format then we would be able to meet our deadlines better without putting pressure on them to meet their deadlines with us. They were very amenable to this, and this is what we now do. The outcome is that we are now able to deliver all reports to them in a timely fashion even when they miss deadlines, and rather than having three people work on this we now do it with only two. This allows us to alternate between the three of us who does this on a monthly basis, and has provided more variety of work for us."

Not only does this response provide evidence of the interviewee making suggestions for changes, it also demonstrates them putting themselves in the shoes of another business area, a willingness to consult with and involve others and recognition of the commercial implications of their thinking. Whilst these areas might not be the ones being assessed by the interviewer in this question, the response provides additional information that either the interviewer or the interviewee can come to in other questions. In terms of **CAR**, the answer provides the following:

- **Circumstances**: preparation of financial reports in a bank where the team was overworked and producing duplicate reports.
- **Action**: suggestions for change to reports, and consultation with internal clients in order to achieve this.
- **Result**: development of a simplified report format that still met the needs of all parties while reducing the workload for the finance team.

USING AN EXAMPLE MORE THAN ONCE

Whilst an interview question is designed to elicit information about a specific competency, most work activities actually involve more than one competency. You'll therefore find it impossible to restrict your answer to only that competency. You do need to emphasise the relevant competency, but you can also come back to the same example and use it differently. A word of warning, though – don't use the same example more than twice. The danger is that you will not demonstrate sufficient breadth of experience.

Middle management level

For a middle management role, the interviewer will be seeking more complexity in the issues that you talk about. Either your examples will need to have a higher level of focus or the issues will need to be more complex and more interrelated, requiring more careful consideration and balancing of implications.

Interviewer: Tell me about a time where you had to anticipate potential problems and how you went about developing contingencies.

 Poor answer:

"Well, that's part of a manager's job really. It's important that I keep on top of what is going on in our market place. I do this by regularly speaking to my contacts and reading the trade press. I have also instigated regular weekly meetings with the team, where we all report back what is happening in the market and this allows us to take corrective action at an early stage. For example, I recently completely restructured my sales team as our competitors were beginning to catch up with us and I needed to take corrective action quickly. The restructure made us more nimble and better placed to beat the competition."

Why is this a poor answer?

The answer starts at a general level. When eventually an example is cited, it is not very detailed or specific. Remember, this is for a middle management role, so an interviewer would be expecting more depth to the response. Had the interviewee followed the CAR principles more closely, we would have a more in depth and detailed response.

 Better answer:

"Yes, as manager of a sales team of ten people, I was becoming increasingly aware of a competitor that was beginning to encroach on our territory. To date, we had not lost sales – our clients were buying both products – but we

obviously needed to ensure that in future this didn't change. The way we were set up as a client team at the time was that different sales people were specialised in different products, and between them covered a very large geographical area. I could see that our competitors were more nimble and I needed to find a way to match this. What I did was to split the big area into five smaller ones and restructure the team such that two sales execs were responsible for each of the smaller areas. This meant that they would also need product training so that they could speak to their clients in a knowledgeable fashion and provide continued good client care. The overall impact of this was that the sales execs developed a more intimate relationship with their customers – they had fewer, and more time with them, and were able to offer them a wider choice of product. They were also more nimble in their response to client needs. This approach counteracted what our competitors were doing and we were able to continue to grow sales."

Whilst this is a short and succinct response, it encapsulates the sort of thought leadership that is expected at this level. It demonstrates an awareness of the need to look outside of the organisation, to be aware of competitors and to position the business, at team level, to respond to a threat.

Clearly, there is much more information for an interviewer to elicit here. Other aspects to be probed could include: the data that was used to drive decision making, who was consulted, the options that were considered, the strengths and weaknesses of those options and the risks that were being taken.

Interviewer: Tell me about a business opportunity that you became aware of and what you did to capitalise on it.

 Poor answer:

"One of my key clients called one day to speak to me about a need that he had. Basically, he needed some support with advice around a redundancy situation that he potentially had to deal with. This is an area of specialism for us, and we were able to support him in both the legal aspects of this to ensure that he did it right, as well as providing some training interventions to support managers who might be losing some of their staff. Finally, there was scope to provide support on the outplacement work. I wrote a proposal outlining our approaches to all three and sent this to him."

For a middle management level, this is a very basic response. In any business development situation, you would expect a response that might include a written proposal. The example does not demonstrate any originality of thought, proactive action or any lasting change. In short it does not demonstrate sufficient thought leadership.

 Better answer:

"I took a call from a client one day with whom I had a really good relationship. We had been working with them for a number of years and providing them with HR services. This was our area of specialism, and he respected our responsiveness and integrity. He also mentioned to me that what I missed was some of the technology that he knew that some of the bigger players in the market were providing, although at much higher cost than us. This led to a discussion around his technology needs. Given that we were not a software house, I started to explore the market to see if there was a potential small IT firm that we could partner with so as to meet the needs of this long-standing client. I sourced a potential partner and worked with them to put together a profit-share model. Armed with this, we were able to meet with my client and discuss how we might be able to support them. This was the first time we had done something like this and the result was that it allowed us to start offering more sophisticated solutions to our clients."

Although this is not an example of proactive action, it demonstrates a willingness to look at a situation and to problem-solve, resulting in more business that later translated into an overall organisational impact. From this perspective it demonstrates leadership in creating a new way of doing things and driving business improvement. It also fits the **CAR** model:

- **Circumstances**: the example provides the context of a pre-existing, good client relationship that has been ongoing for a number of years. It also provides the reason for the client call.
- **Action**: the example then goes on to illustrate what actions the interviewee took in terms of trying to meet the client's needs by exploring possibilities with other technology suppliers.
- **Result**: the interviewee was able to provide more sophisticated IT-based HR solutions.

Interviewer: Can you give me an example of a time where you needed a solution to a problem where no precedent had been set?

✗ Poor answer:

"*We had no career break policy at all, and I knew that career breaks are becoming more popular. I therefore decided that one was needed and drafted out a broad policy that I presented to the senior management team. They thought it was a good idea and I therefore set about writing it in more detail. I put together a proposal outlining the business benefits, as well as outlining a financial model that would help us to better understand what the cost to the business was likely to be.*"

With a bit more detail, this could be a strong answer. There is evidence of proactive action, consultation with other people and a structured approach to introducing the change. The need for change was linked to potential business need and there was talk of an analytical approach. Were the response fuller and given in terms of CAR, it would be much stronger.

✓ Better answer:

"Yes, one of my team wanted to take a career break for six months. As a small business, nobody had requested this before and so we had no systems and processes in place to deal with it. It was Nigel, who had been with us for about 7 years and was a well regarded member of the team, so we wanted to retain him. I say this, because my first thought was he could just resign and then come back. Then I realised that we might not have any vacancies when he returned and we'd lose him. So I spoke to our head of HR, and with him, we drew up a career break policy that would allow people who had been with us for 5 years or more to be entitled to a maximum 6 months' break. Our commitment to them would be that we kept their job open, while their commitment to us would be to return for a minimum of one year after their break. The career break was unpaid. We arrived at this policy because I spoke to some contacts that I have in other organisations to see what they did, and our head of HR looked at it from the employment legislation perspective. The result is that we now have a policy that is popular and has been taken advantage of by a number of staff."

How well do you think this example answers the question? It is structured according to **CAR**:

- **Circumstances**: the need for a new precedent was described.
- **Action**: the interviewee worked with the head of HR to draft a career break policy.
- **Result**: Nigel could take a career break and still be able to return to work afterwards. This action ensured that the business retained a good member of the team whilst at the same time meeting the needs of that team member.

In terms of quality of content, this example shows an ability to problem-solve at the level of looking outside and exploring. It does not provide evidence of starting from a completely blank slate, nor does it show originality or ingenuity in solving a particularly difficult issue, and thus defining precedent on a much broader level. If the interviewee had wanted to demonstrate originality of thought or approach, a different example should have been used, perhaps one where they had researched something for themselves rather than working with somebody else.

CREATIVITY AND INNOVATION IN THE THOUGHT DOMAIN

Interviewees often assume that a response relating to change or problem solving needs to demonstrate innovation or creativity. Indeed, creativity and imagination are two things that interviewees often find difficult and intimidating to respond to. This doesn't need to be the case; the sorts of innovation and creativity that interviewees assume are needed are not what the interviewer is necessarily looking for. Many interviewees place themselves in the 'uncreative box'. This actually limits their thinking and makes responding to such interview questions difficult.

In the work place, creativity is also about using an existing process in a new way or in a different setting – it does not need to be a totally original idea.

Senior management level

For senior management roles, the examples that you give in an interview will need to demonstrate breadth of thinking with a broader focus. At this level, it is likely that decisions will have an impact on a whole business area or even on the organisation as a whole, and that it will be longer lasting. The financial implications are also likely to be bigger. An interviewer will be looking for evidence that issues have been well thought through, that they demonstrate awareness not only of the internal organisational environment but also of external factors, including other organisations, the industry as a whole, the economy and, potentially, the political agenda. As you can see, many factors need to be drawn into the 'thought' domain at this level.

ACTIVITY 6

REVIEW YOUR THOUGHT LEADERSHIP EXPERIENCE

Think of examples that you could give in response to these three questions, based on your experience.

- Describe an occasion when you have initiated significant change in the workplace for the benefit of the organisation.
- Tell me about a time when you have used recent developments in your area to inform your decision making.
- Can you give me an example of where you had to develop a new strategy?

Interviewer: Describe an occasion when you have initiated significant change in the workplace for the benefit of the organisation.

✗ Poor answer:

"*The most recent example would be changes to our pay and remuneration system. It had not been looked at for a number of years, so it was about time that it had an overhaul. I asked HR to carry out a benchmarking exercise for me so that we could get a sense of how we were remunerating our staff compared to our competitors. The analysis showed that many of our competitors were paying more, so obviously we needed to keep up with them. I therefore recommended that we find ways of equalising our pay to the current market conditions. When we evaluated this in our next staff survey we found that staff satisfaction and engagement had increased from the previous year, so it seems to have worked.*"

This is not at all a strong answer. On the surface, decisions and actions seem to be data driven and the results seem to have benefitted the business. The problem, though, is that the thinking is not joined up and the conclusions drawn do not follow from the original premise. The interviewee has not been able to provide an example of a clear antecedent, action and outcome. Changing salaries as a result of a benchmarking exercise is fine, but the increased engagement cannot be linked to this. An interviewer will be looking for clear, rational and data driven decision making, together with an evaluation and outcomes that make sense in the whole context.

✓ Better answer:

"*The most recent example that I can think of is in our pay and remuneration process. We conduct an annual staff survey and I had noticed a trend in the feedback with regard to how people perceived remuneration in the business. This was a tricky one, as people didn't openly discuss it, but the survey indicated that there was a general sense of inequity and a bit of a 'black box' approach to it. It obviously needed addressing, and at one of the senior team meetings I raised this and volunteered to look into it. It was outside of my area as I'm not HR, but I recognised that as someone that was dealing with the commercial realities of the business on a daily basis I could work with the*

HR director to implement some change. The consequences of not doing so could potentially have been a steady stream from our doors to our competitors. So, to cut a long story short, I did some research into what approaches to remuneration were commonplace in our industry, what the perceived upsides and downsides of the different systems were, and with this information worked with our head of HR and some remuneration specialists to devise a new scheme. Our most recent staff survey has shown better results in this area, and our business has continued to grow, despite some difficult trading times."

The above example demonstrates succinctly the initiation of some change that had an impact at the organisational level.

- **Circumstances**: review of staff survey indicated dissatisfaction with remuneration.
- **Action**: the interviewee then describes, in broad terms, what he did, i.e. becoming involved and researching approaches to remuneration.
- **Result**: implementation of a changed process, and staff survey results with more positive feedback from staff.

More generally, the interviewee has demonstrated awareness of internal issues, looking outside the business and using that as a basis for driving change within the business. Overall, the initiative seems to have had a positive impact. More detail is clearly needed in this answer. For example, there is no detail about what changes were actually made and how they were introduced. Information on this would give the interviewer more confidence, as well as providing subsidiary evidence on task- and people-based issues.

Interviewer: Tell me about a time where you have used recent developments in your area to inform your decision making.

 Poor answer:

"It's always important to keep on top of new developments in the field. We actually have a department that deals with this and I often work in close collaboration with them to introduce new products and services. For example, I recently suggested to them that they look at improving our online discussion

forums that we host to support some of our products as I felt there must be more we could do to make them interesting and engaging."

This response really lacks depth at this level. There is some indication of change, but it is presented in a way that suggests it happened as an aside. There is also no real sense of ownership – it's implied that this actually sits with another department and that the interviewee has limited exposure as a result. This may well be the case, but as an interviewee, you need to think about how to make the best of the limited experience that you may have, whilst obviously staying truthful.

Let's look at a better response:

 Better answer:

"Sure, as an IT and internet business, we need to keep on top of the latest developments in the marketplace and ensure that our customers are also kept up to date. As part of our customer service commitment, we run several discussion forums that allow users of our products to keep in touch with not just us, but also each other, and thus discuss their experiences. Our support staff also read these and will from time to time contribute to them. Now, discussion forums are a bit dry and they're not really like a proper discussion at all because everything is completely sequential. Recently, there has been a new development that combines different web communication methods into one allowing both chatroom- and forum-style communication. It has made the process of communicating far more collaborative. Now clearly, this was going to be an entirely different form of keeping in touch with our customers, and from a change perspective, we had to plan both internal and external aspects of this change very carefully. On a broader level, it needed changes in skills and attitude from both our staff and customers and as such was not without its problems."

Again, this response is short, and there is scope for exploring it in much more detail. However, the outlines of a senior management-level response are there. It demonstrates proactive introduction of change, based on an awareness of what is going on outside the business, to drive improvement. The change had both internal and external impact and required the need to address attitudes and skills – a complicated change initiative by anyone's standards.

The response also suggests more involvement and drive from the interviewee than the previous, poorer, answer.

Interviewer: Tell me about a time when you recognised that the current strategy was no longer appropriate.

 Poor answer:

"*As an organisation in business for over 20 years, we had developed an excellent name in the marketplace and frequently our reputation preceded us. As a result, there was relatively little that we needed to do in the form of sales and marketing activity. However, the recession of 2008/2009 put a stop to that. Our order book very quickly began to dry up and there were fewer prospects in our pipeline. Our reliance on having developed intimate relationships with our clients and keeping close to them was, on its own, not going to see us through this difficult period. We needed to become more proactive and we needed to grow a stronger market awareness beyond those clients that we regularly worked with. Fundamentally, we needed a change in strategy. So I suggested to my fellow directors that we needed to re-examine the strategy, as I felt it was no longer effective in the prevailing economic climate.*"

The example is not very strong, it is a little reactive – strategy was changed in response to a drying-up pipeline. At this level, a good candidate needs to be off the mark more quickly and recognise, for example, at the onset of the economic downturn, that current strategy would not be sufficient. Whilst responding differently to the question and indicating that the actions were spontaneous might improve the answer, it is likely that an interviewer would discover this through their probing. A better response would be one that demonstrated proactively addressing a strategic issue.

The interviewer will also be looking for more detail as to exactly how the respondent became aware of the situation, for example, what key indicators they were looking at, and how this compared not just to the previous year, but to other times of economic downturn.

✓ Better answer:

"*As a business, we are over 20 years old, and in that time have developed a really good reputation in the market place, to the extent that we did not have to actively market ourselves. In the recession of 2000, things did slow down a bit but we were still able to meet our targets. When the recession hit in 2008 though, I recognised that we needed to change the way we go to market. It was clear from what was happening in the markets that this recession was going to be much deeper and longer. All the reports were pointing to the fact that a wider sector of industry was going to be affected and it was unlikely that we would escape unharmed. It was obvious that we could not afford to rely on our reputation alone. A rethink of our strategy was therefore needed, so this is what I suggested to the board. I supported this recommendations with some "what if" analyses that showed potential recommendations of not doing anything. These indicated that we would be able to maintain our position for approximately 2 months, but that after that, sales volume would shrink and costs would increase owing to the weakness of sterling to such an extent that we would need to try to look to drastic ways of managing our costs – potentially even redundancies.*"

Why is this response stronger? Action was proactive as well as showing learning from the experience of the previous recession. The respondent also provided evidence of some analysis that was carried out to support the recommendation that made.

In terms of CAR, we have evidence for C and A. It is too soon to have any results, but the answer could have been strengthened by providing information on the indicators that would be looked at to evaluate the outcome in the strategy change.

Interviewer: Tell me about a time when you recognised that change was needed.

"One of our production facilities was not meeting its expected targets. When I explored the underlying reasons for this, it became apparent that the production unit manager hadn't adopted the new ways of working that we had introduced the previous year as part of a general drive to increase production. At the time, she had been hesitant but had agreed to buy into the change and try to make it work. In fairness to her, she was managing a difficult site that had a history of disagreement with senior management. In my discussion with her, though, it had become apparent that she hadn't succeeded in implementing the changes we had discussed and so the facility was falling behind its production targets. This clearly needed to be addressed quickly because it was having an overall impact on the business plan. What we decided to do was to identify those employees that would be supportive of the change and only with them, on certain lines, introduce these new changes. We changed our implementation plan, with the overall aim still being that we would ultimately convert the whole facility. My thinking was that by showing it could work on a small scale in the facility, alongside the successes in other facilities, we might be able to get them on board with what we were proposing."

This example addresses an aspect of organisational change. It demonstrates the respondent's awareness of the change not having lived up to expectations and their willingness to alter the implementation approach so as to make it work.

- **Circumstances**: a change had been introduced which had not yet taken hold in a production facility. Consequently, the facility was underperforming.
- **Action**: identify a small cohort of supportive individuals and introduce the change to them, in the hope that this would then cascade through the unit.
- **Result**: is not provided, as it is too early.

However, do you notice something else about this response?

It's actually an example of a piece of change implementation that has not gone particularly well and, as such, the response shows some negative indicators against managing change. In other words, had the change been managed better from the outset, and in particular given the history of that particular production facility, the challenges encountered might have been avoidable. The interviewee would therefore have been better off choosing an alternative example.

Further practice questions

Look at the questions below and sketch out on paper a broad framework response. Try to make this align with the **CAR** model. The questions are suitable for all levels of role, but you may want to adjust them to provide a better fit for the role you are applying for.

■ Give me an example of a time when you had to analyse a complex (business) problem and make some recommendations.

■ Do you have an example of a time when you analysed some information in order to help you make a decision?

■ Describe an occasion when you have initiated significant change in the workplace for the benefit of the organisation. *Or, for a less senior role:* Describe an occasion when you have made changes to a system or process in order to bring about an improvement.

■ Tell me about a time where you needed to find a solution to a new problem.

■ How do you think the current economic change is impacting our industry, and what changes have you put in place to address those threats? (This question is for senior roles).

ACTIVITY 7

MOCK INTERVIEW

Ask a friend to conduct a mock interview with you and provide you with feedback. Give them some questions – the ones from this section if you struggle to write your own – and practise. Key things to watch out for:

■ Are your responses clear and easy to understand?

■ Was your response full and comprehensive, without rambling or drifting?

■ Did you structure your response according to **CAR**?

■ Were your examples as recent and as varied as possible, to demonstrate breadth of experience?

IN A NUTSHELL

Thought leadership is important at all levels; its importance increases with seniority. A solid response gives the interviewer confidence that you can deal with the intellectual challenges of the role.

- The 'thought' domain is about direction, strategy, creativity, problem solving, change, innovation, judgement and decision making.
- Depending on the seniority of the role, you need to think about the focus of your responses: is it mainly at the individual, team or organisational level?
- Creativity is not always about originality. Creativity can also be demonstrated by applying existing approaches to a new situation.

6 PEOPLE-BASED QUESTIONS

Example Interview Answers

People competencies are often weighted especially highly by organisations' selection processes. References, CV and track record will say a lot about your 'task' and 'thought' competencies without revealing much about your style when it comes to working with and managing people. For this reason you can expect a tough interview to focus strongly on this aspect of your performance. In this chapter we will:

- remind you how to use the **CAR** model to frame your answers

- cover how to recognise people-based questions

- show you how to prepare examples of your people skills

- give you a range of examples of poor and better answers to help you prepare for the 'people' skills part of a competency-based interview.

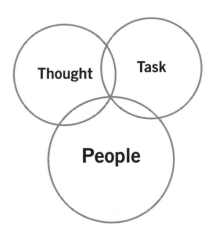

What are employers looking for in terms of people skills?

Businesses know that your 'people' skills are often the key to success, so it is no surprise that they will be particularly interested in how well you work in teams, how well you manage and lead people, how confident and credible you are with customers and how well you develop people.

Interviewers want to know how well you work in teams, manage, lead and develop people, and how credible you are with customers.

At entry and middle levels of recruitment the interviewer will be most interested in your interpersonal skills; at higher levels they will want to see that you think strategically about people issues and that you can build strong teams around you. At all levels they will be interested in issues such as:

- how well you handle conflict
- how you consult, engage and bring people in
- how good you are at influencing
- what your management/leadership style is like
- how self-aware you are

- how flexible your style is – whether can you be democratic or more directive, as the situation needs.

As in the earlier sections, we will use the **CAR** model (Circumstances, Action, Results) as a way of encouraging you to build good answers, so you may want to refer back to Chapter 1 for a quick reminder of how to use this approach. As before, questions and answers will be pitched at different levels and we will go through them to identify the main 'dos' and 'don'ts' of framing strong answers to these tough questions.

Employers will be looking for a range of people skills and balance in your interpersonal style. Choose your examples accordingly.

Recognising people-based questions

Look out for words or phrases like these to help you recognise that the interviewer is looking for a people-based answer:

influence	persuade	inspire	motivate	team
challenge	disagreement	engagement	culture	succession
talent	cooperation	performance management	appraisal	communication
team building	attitudes	personality	personal impact	rapport
credibility	trust			

Questions containing words or phrases like these are likely to require an answer based on your perceptions of people and on your own awareness of your style with other people. People-based questions are trying to get at things such as:

- do you recognise your own impact on other people?
- are you typically cooperative – a team player – or are you more independent?

- perhaps most importantly – will you fit in?

Preparing to respond to people-based questions

We are highly evolved social animals, skilled in making judgements about other people – based, sometimes, on pretty flimsy evidence – so the interviewer will also be interested in your self-awareness and self-presentation during the interview (see Chapter 3). Once again, the words you say and the way you say them will need to join up if you want to leave the interviewer with the best possible impression.

ARE YOU A PEOPLE PERSON?

As well as the preparation already covered in Chapter 2, try to recall examples of situations where you have had to:

- get people to buy in to an idea or process
- pass on a difficult message
- handle interpersonal conflict
- develop/coach a person or a group
- make 'people' decisions, such as who to put in a team
- 'sell' an idea or a product
- plan communication across a wide group of people.

Once again, use the **CAR** process to frame a short description of the example, making sure that you cover the circumstances, the action you took and the results.

EXAMPLE INTERVIEW ANSWERS

Graduate/trainee management level

Interviewer: Can you give me an example of a time when you have had to deal with an interpersonal conflict or disagreement in a team?

✗ Poor answer:

"*There was a time in the design team when one of the senior designers was causing a real problem. It was his attitude really; he was very critical of everyone else's work – even if it had nothing to do with him – but was very unwilling to take any criticism of his own stuff. The juniors were getting very de-motivated. In the end we had to get the head of marketing to have a word and he did improve a bit. I think he was insecure, basically, he still doesn't share his own ideas but at least he has stopped criticising everyone else.*"

This is not a good example of a people-based answer. There is no sign of what interpersonal skills were brought to bear to tackle the situation, nor is there any evidence relating to this person's approach to dealing with conflict. Indeed, what evidence there is, is negative! For example:

- the outcome is hardly positive
- the action was to get someone else to tackle the issue
- there is no evidence of getting to the root of the problem
- there is some evidence of avoiding the difficult conversation rather than tackling it.

By asking a 'people' question the interviewer is looking for evidence that you can deal with difficult conversations; they will not be reassured by this answer.

✓ Better answer:

"*There was a time in the design team when one of the senior designers was causing a real problem. His style was quite abrasive; he was very critical of the work of some of the junior designers, to the point that they had started avoiding him. It was bad for team morale and it meant that they weren't getting the benefit of his design expertise. While I wasn't his manager, I decided to have a quiet word with him – I wanted to see if he was aware of the impact he was having on people. It turned out that he was under a lot of pressure himself and that a lot of his criticism was the result of his not having time to think through the feedback properly. He really didn't seem to be aware of just how rude he sounded when he was under this kind of time pressure. I think making him aware of it was half the battle, and while he was a bit 'off' about my feedback initially, he agreed that team morale was really important. What he now does is to set aside review time with the juniors rather than them just firing designs at him as they are completed. This seems to be working and the team seems a lot happier.*"

Circumstances, action and result are much more clearly explained here.

- **Circumstances**: a problem individual who was causing friction.
- **Action**: taking the initiative in speaking to the individual.
- **Result**: the individual changed his behaviour.

As a result, the interviewer will be in a much better position to judge this person's people skills. In particular:

- the person recognised that there was a people problem
- they didn't shy away from a potentially difficult conversation
- the people issue was tackled in a professional way
- the issue was viewed from both sides – the manager's and the juniors'
- the good of the team was a clear motivation for action
- the result seems to have been good.

People-based questions are often trying to get an assessment of your emotional intelligence. In other words, how well you understand yourself, how well you understand other people and how well you can flex your style to have the impact you want in a particular situation. This answer ticks a lot of these boxes.

Interviewer: Can you tell me about a time when you had to 'sell' an idea or new concept to a group of people?

(This example is one that is frequently asked as a part of structured interviews).

 Poor answer:

"*There was a time when the team I was supervising in the call centre were very resistant to a new shift pattern that was being introduced. It didn't affect their overall hours but the start and finish times were slightly different – only by half an hour. Call centre staff are notorious for being picky about any change in routine and I knew there would be a lot of moaning. What I did was to get them all together in their shift teams and let them sound off before I explained that this change applied to everyone and that they would soon get used to it. It took a couple of weeks but they soon settled in to the new routine.*"

Not much sign of emotional intelligence or interpersonal sensitivity here! A particular problem with this answer (amongst many) is the tone used to describe people and their feelings. Phrases like – 'I let them sound off' and 'a lot of moaning' do not sound respectful or sensitive to their issues. 'Notorious for being picky' also sends out the wrong signal, suggesting that all staff are the same and that it is OK to stereotype them. In short, the answer again provides negative evidence about people skills. Remember – a people question demands a people-based answer. This answer is very task focused – it doesn't tell the interviewer much about how you sell ideas or influence people; in fact, it sends out a message that the person is somewhat insensitive.

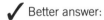 Better answer:

"*When I was supervising the call centre team, the need arose to change the shift pattern to bring it in line with other sections. I could see that this would need discussing with the team because it might have an impact on their domestic arrangements, pick-up times and so on. Once the memo explaining the change had come through from HR, I spoke to everyone in turn, picking them up during their breaks. I wanted to hear of any concerns from them personally – better than doing it in a group where some people might be nervous about speaking up. There were some worries, but I tried to reassure*

them on a case-by-case basis, I made it clear that they still had flexi-time available as a way of smoothing out anything that was particularly difficult in terms of hours. I also tried to sell the positives; the new shift pattern would help people to avoid peak travel periods. Doing it this way seemed to work, because no one raised any grievances and the new pattern was in place without too much trouble."

You can see **CAR** at work in this answer.

- **Circumstances**: a problematic change of shift pattern in a call centre.
- **Action**: deciding to speak to each person individually.
- **Result**: no grievances and the new pattern was in place with little trouble.

Just as importantly, you can see the person responding to the 'human' side of the question. The answer shows recognition of concerns, a well thought-through approach to how to sell the idea (one to one rather than in a group), and emphasis on the positives as a way of gaining agreement. From this answer the interviewer can tell that this person is thinking through the 'people' implications of the change and has exercised sound judgement as to the best way of communicating the change.

Middle management level

As the level of the interview goes up, so will the interviewer's expectations about the scope of your 'people' competencies. At middle management level they will be interested in questions such as:

- Can this person balance and resolve competing interests or motives?
- How does this person communicate/motivate across teams?
- Do they think more widely about people issues, encompassing things like training and development and talent management?
- How well do they manage 'upwards', how do they engage with different groups of people – peers, managers and subordinates?

Interviewer: Can you tell me about a time when you have had to communicate a tough decision about an individual or team? How did you go about it?

 Poor answer:

"OK, well after the merger at my last job, it was clear that the marketing department was overstaffed and that we would have to make some redundancies. I have always believed that 'clean and fast' is the best way of communicating this kind of news so I took a lot of time to draft a letter to each individual explaining that jobs were at risk and describing the process we were going to go through in detail. I got a lot of help from HR because it's so important to get the details right. I made sure that everyone got the letter on their desks at the same time and I made it clear that HR would be available to deal with any questions that they had."

This is a task-based answer – it says what the person did but it does not pick up on the subtleties of human communication and behaviour that the interviewer is really interested in. Interpersonal style does not come through and the interviewer is going to have to ask a lot of follow-up questions to get at this detail. There is also a risk that, having noted the task-based approach to the issue, the interviewer will be looking for evidence that this is indeed the emphasis of this person's style and that the more subtle emotional intelligence skills are missing; in other words, the interviewer will now check for still more negative evidence. Let's see what happens with the probe questions.

Interviewer: So how did people respond?

✗ Poor answer:

"*Well, clearly people were concerned; I could see a lot of worried faces around the office but at least everyone knew where they stood.*"

Interviewer: Did this affect performance?

✗ Poor answer:

"*I don't think so; HR did a good job of explaining the timing and that the process would be fair and transparent.*"

Interviewer: So how many people did you lose, what was the reaction of those who stayed?

✗ Poor answer:

"*We lost five in the end and the four who stayed have reallocated the workload so that the marketing plan is still pretty much on track.*"

At this point the interviewer is likely to give up on trying to get this person to describe the human elements of the situation. They will conclude that the person is task focused but is not showing any signs of recognising the motivational issues or the personal sensitivities of the individuals in the team. So what does the interviewer actually want to hear in this situation? Some of the key elements they need to hear in the answer include:

■ recognition that people's feelings and apprehensions matter in this situation
■ recognition that a 'people' response has been made to a 'people' problem; for example communicating, talking, understanding, engaging, supporting
■ that different options have been considered based on an understanding of people's likely reactions and recognising the need to keep the marketing function running smoothly
■ that there is some sign of interpersonal sensitivity, and awareness of how people will be feeling.

'People' answers do not have to be 'soft and fluffy' – the interviewer will want to hear a degree of objectivity being applied – but at the same time the answers do need to make reference to the issues listed above. Otherwise the risk is that the interviewer will come to the conclusion that this person does not 'do' people. As a result, scores on the people competencies are likely to be low.

✓ Better answer:

"OK, well after the merger at my last job it was clear that the marketing department was overstaffed and that we would have to make some redundancies. This is never easy, so I first spoke to HR to make sure that the process was crystal clear. We drafted a letter explaining all the details but I wanted to communicate the change personally, so I decided that I would call a meeting with the marketing team to tell them myself and then hand out the letters to cover all the detail. I wanted to let them know that we recognised how difficult this would be and that we hadn't made the decision lightly."

Interviewer: So how did people respond?

"I think telling them face to face paid off. Clearly they were concerned, but they were able to ask questions there and then – I didn't want bad information to start all kinds of rumours going – I had Brian from HR with me, so between us we were able to answer all their questions about the process and about timing. Interestingly, a lot of the concerns were about how ongoing projects could be finished. I thought that said a lot about the dedication of the team."

This sequence pushes a lot of important buttons in terms of 'people' answers and it is worth reviewing them.

- It recognises the importance of the 'personal touch'; communication in a difficult situation is handled face to face rather than impersonally. This is not to say that face to face is always better, but in the context of this question it shows that the person is not shying away from a challenging interpersonal situation.
- There is recognition of the 'human nature' aspects of the situation; people's fears and concerns are acknowledged and a rationale for dealing with them is explained – all provide signs of the emotional intelligence that the interviewer is looking for.

- Names are used; 'Brian' is referred to by name and this sends out an important signal that you are dealing with people and not with 'production units'. Using names makes your answer sound much more personal and suggests that you are interested in relationships.
- Good qualities of the team are referred to – 'dedication'; seeing the good in people is an important way of indicating that you are thoughtful about things like team dynamics, personal motivations – in other words, that you care about people issues.

When answering people questions you need to balance objectivity with evidence that you are thoughtful about the 'softer' issues. The best way of doing this is to make sure that your answers contain words relating to motivation, feelings, attitudes, concerns and all the stuff that makes people what they are.

If you are the kind of person who is naturally objective and tough minded, then review your examples with a view to taking the perspective of other people in the situation.

If you are the kind of person who naturally sees the human side of things, then make sure you do not sound too 'soft and fluffy'; the best way of doing this is to relate the people issues back to business performance.

Interviewer: Can you tell me how you go about managing your team in your current role? Give me an example of how you run your meetings.

✗ Poor answer:

"*I'm really lucky in the current finance team; they are really motivated and enthusiastic so I don't have to do very much in terms of inspiring them. They are all very different characters but they get on really well. We have weekly meetings and I keep the agenda very open; anyone can raise anything they like – I find this encourages new ideas and problem solving – and I make sure that everyone has a chance to speak. I suppose you could summarise my management style by saying that I try to be very supportive; I can't remember the last time I had to throw my weight around – they know what needs doing, they gel, and the work gets done.*"

Superficially this looks like a very people-based answer, but there are some real risks with the 'I am a very nice person' approach. In most interviews, particularly at managerial level, the interviewer will be looking for evidence of *balance* in your managerial style. Earlier we mentioned the value of showing that you can flex your style to meet the needs of the situation, and this is not apparent in the answer above. The interviewer is going to have to ask a lot more questions to see if this person has anything other than a laissez-faire management style.

Interviewer: So how do you check that people know what they need to do?

 Poor answer:

"*It's mostly a matter of having an open door so that people can check things with me; anything they are unsure about, I make sure I am available.*"

Interviewer: So what about when you have to be more directive, can you give me an example of how you handle this?

 Poor answer:

"*I suppose there are situations when the requirement is non-negotiable and obviously then I let people know what they have to do by when. I can remember times when it looked as if we were going to miss a deadline or where there was an urgent request for information, and in this kind of situation I can give clear instructions if I have to.*"

Eventually we get to some reference to a more directive style of management, but it still falls far short of being a concrete example and the whole sequence will leave the interviewer doubtful about this person's ability to behave in a more directive way when the situation requires it.

 Better answer:

"I'm really lucky in my current finance team, they're motivated and there are no real weak links. They're all very different characters but they can all be relied on to deliver high quality work. I split my weekly meetings into two sections. First there is a progress and issues review where we all keep track of the current workload and look ahead to see what workload is coming. Second, I try to give at least half an hour to an 'open agenda' session where people can raise ideas or concerns. My broad approach to management is to make sure that the team are clear about their objectives and then to support them – keeping them on track when necessary – but generally I prefer a 'light touch' when possible. Clearly, if the pressure is on or if there is a problem I will intervene – pretty quickly, usually – because it doesn't help the team or me if we deliver late. The feedback we get is that we are the most efficient finance team in the business, so the approach seems to work."

This answer covers the ground in terms of **CAR**.

- **Circumstances**: a good team, different characters, but a need to manage them.
- **Action**: two activities are described – 'first', 'second'.
- **Result**: 'the feedback we get is that we are the most efficient finance team …'

There are still improvements that could be made, however (think back to our comments on earlier examples), to make this answer richer still.

- Describing what has been done to develop the team will give the interviewer insight into management style.
- An illustration of management style would be good, dropping in a 'for instance' to make the general comments more concrete.
- The interviewer asks for an example of a management meeting – picking a good example of such a meeting and describing it would answer the question.
- Naming and describing – briefly – some of the individuals in the team to make the answer more personal.
- Giving an example of 'intervening' would enable the interviewer to hear what the interviewee did and why.

As we noted in earlier sections, you will need to judge the level and scope of your answers, based on the interview situation you find yourself in. In general, however, mid-level managerial interviewers will expect to see that your people skills extend beyond your personal social skills, to include topics such as:

- cross-team communication
- succession planning
- developing talent
- building and harnessing the right skills
- influencing, persuading and selling.

Our final example looks at a question that explores people skills in the context of a customer-facing, selling situation.

Interviewer: Can you tell me about a time when you had to deal with a difficult conversation or a complaint from a customer?

 Poor answer:

"*Well obviously we work hard to avoid this kind of situation arising but occasionally we do have to sort out a customer problem. There was an issue on the Leeds project when it became clear that we were not going to meet the delivery deadline for the new phone system – not our fault, our suppliers had made a mistake. When the customer called I insisted on taking it because I knew it would be a tricky conversation. Sure enough, she was livid. I had to let her sound off for about 5 minutes – she was being completely unreasonable – before I could get a word in.*"

Interviewer: So what did you do?

 Poor answer:

"*I explained the situation – that our suppliers had let us down – and that we were chasing the order as hard as we could but that it would be another 5 days before we could deliver.*"

Interviewer: So why were they so upset?

 Poor answer:

"*I'm not sure really, as far as I knew the delay didn't have much impact on their schedule, they weren't due to move into the building for another 3 weeks anyway.*"

Interviewer: So what was the outcome?

 Poor answer:

"*She calmed down eventually; I promised that I was giving the matter my personal attention and that I'd see if I could offer some kind of discount to make up for the delay.*"

As well as some clear mistakes – which you should be practised at spotting by now ('I had to let her sound off') – the answer misses a lot of opportunities to show the people skills that the interviewer is looking for. For example:

- Where is the evidence of recognition of the customer's position?
- Where is the evidence of exploring, questioning or engaging with the customer to understand their position?
- Where is the evidence of using or building a relationship with the customer?

There are lots of missed opportunities here; the interviewer will only go so far in probing for the words they want to hear; words like 'understand', 'sympathise', or even 'sorry'. These are the words that would indicate that the 'human' aspects of the situation were understood. As it is, they are missing, and it is not the interviewer's job to give you the benefit of the doubt. Back to our mantra – a 'people' question needs a people-based answer, not a procedural or tasked-based response.

✓ Better answer:

"Well obviously we work hard to avoid this kind of situation arising but occasionally we do have to sort out a customer problem. There was an issue on the Leeds project when it became clear that we were not going to meet the delivery deadline for the new phone system – not our fault, our suppliers had made a mistake. I took the decision to call the customer myself to apologise and explain – much better than waiting for them to call, and anyway it was the courteous thing to do. At first I was surprised at how upset she was, but when I explored the problem with her a bit it turned out that she had been hoping to bring the occupation deadline forward – it was going to embarrass her with her boss. I asked her if there was anything we could do to help – for example there was a system with a different spec that we could have made available sooner. We talked about putting this offer on the table with her boss so as to help manage her expectations. In the end we agreed to wait for the original equipment. The important thing was to keep the relationship on a good footing, rather than leaving the customer with a sense of having been let down by us."

Why is this a better answer? Apart from its being much fuller and richer, look at the words and the language being used: explain, apologise, courteous, upset, hoping, embarrass, help, expectations, relationship. 'People' words for a 'people' answer!

Senior management level

At this level of interview the scope will be wider still and the interviewer will want evidence that you can think about people issues across the organisation. Issues such as:

- communication between divisions
- strategies for establishing 'people' processes across a business
- high-level influencing
- establishing and retaining relationships with affected parties.

In our experience, interviewers at this level are particularly concerned about the kinds of relationships you will build with peers and other related parties, so your answers need to recognise the 'process' part of people leadership, while still retaining the sense of authenticity that comes from using personal examples.

Interviewer: Earlier you mentioned the merger with ABC Ltd. How did you go about building relationships across the new divisions?

✗ Poor answer:

"*My feeling is that the personal touch is essential here. We had a launch party for the new firm and as head of the legal function I made sure that I touched base with all my peers from across the business. I knew I probably wouldn't get a chance to meet them again for months, so I wanted to be sure that we had at least said 'hello'. I also made sure that I got 5 minutes with the MD, so that it would be easier to catch up again later – it's much easier to take a call from someone whose voice you recognise – and I got his agreement that the legal department would be at the top of the list when it came to the round of departmental meetings he was setting up. In the current situation he could see this made sense because of all the contract negotiations coming up. My aim was to get my credibility built early on so that he would feel he was in safe hands.*"

While there are some good things in this answer, for example the 'personal touch' in building credibility, it's just not systematic enough to 'sell' high-level people skills to the interviewer. As well as getting a fix on your ability to network at an 'event', the interviewer would have been hoping for a lot more evidence of a well thought-through approach to relationship building.

✓ Better answer:

"*Personal contact is clearly important – and I made full use of the launch party to introduce myself to some of the key individuals that I'd be working most closely with – but it was also important that I created some forums where the legal heads could get together – partly to get to know each other better but also to make sure that topics like continuing professional development and international standards were on the agenda. I wanted to quickly create a situation where there were no territorial barriers to our communicating flexibly and quickly when the situation needed it. We've had three legal heads meetings now and they're proving to be a valuable way of making sure that we're sending consistent messages into the business. I've always had a strong relationship with Alison, the MD, and I used this to let her know what I was doing so that she could use the forum to communicate with us as well.*"

This is a much more 'corporate' answer. The human touch is still here, but there is also a focus on organisation-wide people issues, such as communication and development.

We will take one more example, one where the question is more about interpersonal style.

Interviewer: The team you would be leading has been together for a long time now; can you give me an example of a situation where you have had to integrate yourself in this way?

✗ Poor answer:

"My feeling is that you have to clear the air straight away so that people know exactly where you're coming from. When I was parachuted in as head of marketing at ABC Ltd I knew that it was going to be tough getting them to accept me. My remit was – quite frankly – to knock some heads together because business performance had been so poor. At my first meeting I decided that a 'hard but fair' approach was going to work best, so I made it clear that performance was going to be the only yardstick that I was interested in. I'm very open and honest in my style – I think it's the only way you can build trust at senior level – and I think they did find me quite blunt for the first 3 months, but it got results."

This is certainly an honest answer but it falls into a category of 'all or nothing' responses. What it does not show is any degree of subtlety or flexibility. The 'I am what I am' approach is courageous but risky, because its success depends on this person's style happening to fit the circumstances. What if the team to be led are already high performing? What if they are delivering great results under a lot of pressure and need support rather than 'hard but fair'?

✓ Better answer:

"At ABC Ltd it was clear that I was entering a difficult situation; I had taken some soundings from other department heads and they told me that the team was having a tough time at the moment and that they were underperforming. My approach was to have one-to-one meetings with all the marketing directors to find out what the true situation was and get a sense for how people were feeling. I didn't want to go barging in without having some sense for the team's capability, and the meetings helped a lot. I didn't have a lot of time, given the pressure we were under but that original investment in getting to know them paid off, they were working in silos and I had to get them talking to each other. I eventually moved a couple of the directors to other roles, but because I had got to know the team, people could see the rationale for my decisions and

it has helped to create a much more motivated group. I've taken the same approach with the new people I've brought in – encouraging them to have one-to-ones as well, and the result has been a much faster turnaround than if I hadn't invested that time."

The interviewer will get the following message from this answer:

- it takes account of both 'soft' and 'hard' factors
- the focus is on getting to know people before jumping to conclusions
- objective actions are taken, but on the basis of understanding people's capabilities
- expectations are set for how people should behave with each other
- time is invested in people.

At senior level in particular, where time is spent provides a very good measure of an individual's orientation in terms of task, thought and people, so signalling that you make time for people sends an important message.

IN A NUTSHELL

People competencies are highly prized and will be assessed by *what you say and how you say it* (see Chapter 3). Bear the following in mind as you prepare to respond to people-based questions:

- Make sure that you can recognise when the interviewer is focusing on the people domain.
- Showing high-level people competencies is about showing that you have the emotional intelligence to work well with and through people, getting the best from them.
- Think of examples of 'difficult' interpersonal situations or relationships you have encountered; this is a common area of questioning.
- Show that you can think companywide and long term, in terms of the people domain.

7 NON-COMPETENCY-BASED QUESTIONS – BUT STILL TOUGH!

Example Interview Answers

You can't always rely on the interviewer to follow the professional processes we have described in this book. Sometimes a 'favourite' question will slip in, or sometimes, especially in panel interviews, one of the interviewers will decide to go 'off piste' and test you with a question that is hard to relate to a specific competency. In this chapter we will:

■ explore the range of questions that might come up

■ show examples of specific questions

■ give you some 'dos' and 'don'ts' in terms of how to handle them.

Dealing with non-competency-based questions

Your best weapon in dealing with non-competency-based questions is still to identify what the question is trying to get at: is it task, thought or people, or a combination of the three?

- You may be asked questions designed to test your specific knowledge or understanding of a topic or issue, or aimed at assessing how well you know a particular field or market.
- You may be asked hypothetical questions – such as what you might do in a particular situation, or very vague, general questions such as 'Tell me about your leadership style'.
- You may be asked self-disclosure or self-evaluation questions such as 'What is the biggest mistake you have made in the last 3 years, what did you learn from it?', or 'What is your proudest achievement over the last 3 years?'

All the principles we have covered so far still apply to this kind of questioning, specifically:

- If they don't ask you for an example, try to illustrate your answer with real-life instances anyway.
- Use **CAR** to frame your answers.
- If you are asked a hypothetical question, respond by relating it to a real-life experience.
- Get at the gist of the question by using 'task, thought, people' to analyse the questioner's intent.
- Don't be afraid to clarify and reframe the question if appropriate, but check that you have understood their meaning. Answer their question, not the one you would like to answer.

Get at the gist of the question by using 'task, thought, people' to analyse the questioner's intent.

The examples that follow can't cover all the possible questions you might be asked, but they aim to illustrate some of the more common non-competency questions and give you some ideas about how to answer them well. The best advice we can give – experience tells us that it fits in with the interviewer's mindset – is to consider the 'task, thought, people' elements of the question and cover them all in your answer.

CV and chronology-based questions

While less common than used to be the case, interviewers will sometimes want to take you through your CV in some detail. This approach is often used by head hunters as part of their screening; they don't want to put you in front of their client if there are gaps or inconsistencies in your experience.

The interviewer will be trying to understand two things as part of this process; the first, as indicated above, is a straightforward accuracy check; the second is to understand the roles you have had in more detail.

CV checking

Before going for your interview, it obviously makes sense for you to have recently read your own CV! You do not want to sound unsure or uncertain about what you did and when. If there are any gaps or periods of unemployment in your work history, you should not sound embarrassed or defensive about them. Your best course is to show how you made positive use of the time.

Ideally, the interviewer will want to see a steady progression in your roles and responsibilities, but for most people careers are seldom so neat and linear. We all make bad choices occasionally and don't stay in a job for as long as we expected. Again, avoid sounding defensive and instead emphasise the positives that you took from any role, rather than sounding negative and full of regret.

If your CV contains a number of relatively short appointments you may be worried that the interviewer will see you as a 'job hopper' and take it as a sign of a lack of commitment or tenacity. The answer, again, is to be as honest as you can and to explain the situation and, most importantly, what you learned. The interviewer will not be impressed if you seem to have made the same mistake over and over again! Show that you have been thoughtful about what went wrong, that you have learned from it and that your approach is now different in some relevant way. For example:

"*Yes, the two roles in marketing didn't work out as I had hoped. I think my mistake was to go for relatively small organisations where my experience of setting up marketing systems didn't fit their very reactive way of working. I think I managed to add value in both roles in the relatively short time I was there – I still have good relationships with those teams – but I did learn that a larger marketing function suits my skills better."*

Chronology

Broader chronology questions aim to understand the choices you have made in your life, your achievements, your interests and enthusiasms, and how/why your experience has grown in the way it has. Interviewers will vary in terms of how far back they want you to go, but it is not uncommon for them to begin with your education, in order to understand how your interests and expertise got started. In all these questions it is better to sound purposeful rather than the victim of random circumstances. In fact, most of us have careers that have 'accidental' elements to them – we happened to meet someone or 'a friend suggested it' – the trick is to sound as if we exerted positive choices at key points.

More commonly, the interviewer will go through your jobs in chronological order, asking some or all of these questions about each role:

- Why did you decide to take this job?
- What were your main responsibilities/accountabilities?
- Who were your key customers/interested parties?
- What were your most significant achievements?
- What budget were you responsible for?
- How many people were in your team?
- Why did you decide to leave?

Now this can start to sound like a cross-examination, but your responses should be based on all the principles we have discussed so far:

- answer clearly and succinctly; avoid sounding vague about facts
- emphasise positives, not negatives; avoid 'I only had three people in the team' or 'the budget was much smaller than I would have liked'
- prepare; you should at the very least think through what you regard as key achievements in the main roles you have had; phrase your answer using **CAR**.

These questions are designed to assess your experience and your past responsibilities in terms of how closely they fit the job you are applying for and it is worth considering, during your preparation, how good this fit is. Large mismatches will worry the interviewer – they won't necessarily rule you out, but they will reduce the interviewer's confidence in the decision they are making about you. For example, if the role you are applying for has responsibility for managing a budget in the millions and your previous experience has been for budgets in the thousands, you may want to think of ways in which you can plausibly close the gap. For example:

"*But I also sat on the finance committee and there we had oversight of turnover for the whole group, over £18 million when I left.*"

KNOWLEDGE-BASED QUESTIONS

We can't give you right and wrong answers to these questions, they will depend on your particular expertise but there are some general guidelines that should help you frame good answers.

Tell me what you think of the current state of the low-rental social housing market.

Clearly this is designed to assess how well you know this topic and, let's face it, either you do or you don't! Therefore there is little point giving you a model answer. But there are some simple tips you can follow as you build your answers to this kind of question.

■ Your best response is to answer the question based on your knowledge of the subject area. These questions are often asked by a subject-matter expert who may not expect you to know as much as they do, but do avoid getting into a knowledge battle where you are disputing facts with the interviewer. These battles are hard to win in an interview situation. While it is OK to politely disagree with a point that has been put to you, avoid confrontation at all costs!

■ In answering these more technical questions, start with general points and then work down to more specific details, but don't spend more than a couple of minutes on any one answer. If they want more detail they can drill down for it.

■ Be honest about the boundaries of your knowledge, rather than trying to waffle. But rather than just give up and say 'I don't know', share what relevant knowledge you do have. So, for the example question above you might say: *'I haven't had a lot of experience of the social housing sector but my experience as an estate agent tells me that supply is likely to be a significant issue ...'* Where you can, tell them what you do know rather than what you don't know, as long as this doesn't take you off the point.

■ Be willing to take a few moments to pull your thoughts together, rather than blurt out an answer. Signal to the questioner that this is what you are doing by using phrases like *'That's an important question, let me think about it for a second'*, or *'There are alot of factors to consider here, let me just collect my thoughts ...'*

- If you have strong views on the subject raised, make sure that they are well thought through and that you can fully defend them. Avoid sounding too vehement or dogmatic. As a rule of thumb, the more strongly you feel about the topic, the more measured you need to be in the way you talk about it, in order to avoid sounding opinionated.
- Don't pretend that you know something that you don't. Being caught out on a technicality will leave a very bad impression.
- Aim to leave the impression that you are thoughtful and well informed about the subject area, rather than over-confident or even smug!

Hypothetical questions

There are a lot of reasons why these are not good questions for an interviewer to use, but they do still crop up. The main reasons why they are not very effective are that:

- they can assess only your intentions, not your actual behaviour
- they play into the hands of people who are verbally fluent but who may not actually possess the competencies under consideration.

So, what is the best way to handle this kind of question?

Tell me what you would do if you saw a customer abusing one of your staff.

The first step is to assess whether this is primarily a task-, thought- or people-based question; in this instance it is almost certainly a people-based question (though the intent of hypothetical questions can be hard to identify). A big temptation when faced with this kind of question is to say 'Well, it depends …', or to ask a lot of clarifying questions, such as:

- How angry are they?
- Are there other people around?
- What form is the abuse taking, is it verbal or physical?

These are all valid questions (and another good reason why hypothetical questions don't work very well – they are not clear enough), but they run the risk of your frustrating the interviewer. It is better to give your answer based on some sensible assumptions about the situation.

So you might answer as follows:

"*Well, assuming the abuse was verbal, I would intervene, probably saying something like 'is there a problem?' or 'can I help?' My aim would be to take any heat out of the situation once I knew what the problem was.*"

The very best way of tackling this kind of question is to then relate your answer to a real-life example, giving the interviewer concrete evidence – even though they were not professional enough to ask for it!

For example:

"In fact something very similar to this happened to me when I was working at ABC Ltd; one of my colleagues was being shouted at by a customer so I went over and asked if I could help; the customer turned to me to explain, which gave my colleague a few moments to collect her thoughts. I didn't want the customer to think we were ganging up on him, so once things had calmed down I quietly withdrew. I spoke to my colleague afterwards and she said that the pause in the argument had made all the difference."

This answer, relating the question to real experience, gives a much more convincing illustration of your behaviour in this kind of situation. It also lets you apply the tried and tested **CAR** approach to building your answer. It is hard to do this if you are limited to the hypothetical scenario provided by the questioner.

There is a particular subset of hypothetical questions that focuses on the role you are applying for. It usually sounds something like this:

So tell me what you would aim to do in your first 3 months in this job.

It is well worth thinking through answers to this kind of question, depending on the role you are applying for. Make sure that you factor task, thought and people into the proposal you describe. You may have well researched views about what would be required and how you would make a difference, but the chances are that you will not know as much about the situation as the interviewer does. For this reason the following tips are likely to help in framing answers to the question in the above example:

- Emphasise learning, surveying the territory, getting an in-depth understanding, researching.
- Emphasise getting to know key involved parties, understanding roles and sensitivities.

- Emphasise using the above to quickly form a plan; if you have enough information, suggest tentative milestones or objectives for your first 3 months, 6 months and year.
- Sound purposeful but not arrogant in terms of your understanding of the situation.

Tips for hypothetical questions

- Do answer the question, but get the interviewer back to a concrete example as quickly as you can.
- Don't make your answer too elaborate; there is a risk of joining in with the fantasy and embellishing the scenario, giving answers to a whole range of possible outcomes. Keep your answer simple and then try to steer things back onto firmer ground.
- If the question is particularly vague, be willing to ask for some clarification, but don't sound as if you are trying to put the interviewer on the spot – this will not serve you well.
- For this kind of question it is particularly important to give yourself time to think; don't be afraid to buy yourself a few seconds by creating a pause, for example, *'That's an interesting situation, let me think for a second ...'*
- Bring your answer to a clear end, rather than letting it drift off; say something like *'Does that give you enough information?'* as a way of signalling that you have finished the story.

Vague or general questions

These can take many forms, but they are usually characterised by their sheer 'size' and the scope they give you for sounding vague. For example:

- 'Tell me about your approach to financial planning.'
- 'What do you think about change management?'
- 'What is your view about our proposed merger plans?'
- 'Describe your leadership style for me.'
- 'What do you think you would bring to the role you are applying for?'

Once again, we can't give you answers for all these questions, but there are some principles you can apply to add some clarity to your answers. We will use the last example – a too commonly asked question – to illustrate.

What do you think you would bring to the role you are applying for?

The temptation here is to launch into a long list of your personal attributes, for example:

"*Well, I'm proactive, I think I'm pretty good with people, my experience seems very relevant to your situation, I'm good at planning ... etc*"

This scattergun approach is unlikely to differentiate you from other applicants; a better approach is to stick to a few key themes based on your understanding of the competencies they are looking for. At the same time, try to make sure that you cover task, thought and people in your answer. Just because they have asked a very unstructured question does not mean that you cannot give a more focused answer. For example:

"*Well, my understanding of the role is that setting up the new department is the key objective and that you are very sensibly looking for competencies related to making this happen quickly. I believe my planning skills will be important – I've had a lot of experience in project management – I believe my broad awareness of the market will help me to shape the department and make it customer facing and I know the people management skills that*

I learned at ABC Ltd – during the merger – will be essential to developing the team and keeping their morale up in what is going to be a challenging situation."

Task, thought, people and a structure that relates your attributes to the job at hand.

This answer also makes use of the 'rule of three'. This is a rhetorical trick often used by politicians to give emphasis and weight to the point they are making, namely listing three ideas, or three actions or three attributes. In an interview, listing three is a good guide; listing more attributes than this risks losing impact. The rule of three also helps you to maintain your own focus and appear more focused to the interviewer as you give your answer.

Try to make sure that you use language that is as concrete as you can; 'I believe' or better still 'I know' has more impact than 'I think'.

Tips for vague or general questions

- Provide your own structure for your answer; use 'task, thought, people' both to interpret the question and to shape your answer.
- Use the 'rule of three' to add focus.
- Be willing to clarify if the question is particularly vague. For example: *'That's a big question, is there any particular element you would like me to focus on?'*

Self-evaluation, self-disclosure and motivation questions

Sometimes you will be asked to self-asses or to self-disclose as a means for the interviewer to discover how objective or how thoughtful you are about your own performance. They are often trying to assess your honesty with such questions, so an answer that is too glib or immodest risks leaving the wrong impression. Examples of these questions are given below, with poor and better answers.

Self-evaluation questions

- What do you see as your main strengths and weaknesses as far as leadership is concerned?
- Given what you know about this job, where do you see you have most to learn?
- Tell me what you are like at your worst.

✗ Poor answer:

"Well I don't really think I have any 'worst days', my performance is pretty consistent!"

At best, this answer sounds arrogant; at worst, it risks sounding as if you have little self-insight.

✓ Better answer:

"Well, I try to make sure it doesn't happen often but when I am under a lot of pressure I do tend to be a bit less accessible to my team, it doesn't usually last for long and they know they have permission to tell me when I'm doing it!"

This answer admits to a human failing that the interviewer will recognise (and probably share), that is forgivable and that shows you have self-awareness.

Self-disclosure questions

- What do you think is the biggest mistake you made in your last job, what did you learn from it?
- What are you proudest of in what you have achieved in the last 2 years?
- Where would you hope to be in 3 years' time?

✗ Poor answers:

"Well I'm not sure really, I want to see how I get on here first."

"I think by then I'll be ready for a role in a bigger organisation."

"Doing your job."

These are all awful responses, pretty much guaranteed to make you sound unfocused, uninterested or glib.

 Better answer:

"Hopefully making a strong contribution to the business in this role or an expanded role, depending on how quickly I progress. I'm ambitious, but clearly I'll need to establish myself first."

This answer manages to signal ambition and a desire to progress, without sounding arrogant; importantly, it also makes it clear that you want to grow in this business and you are not seeing it as just a stepping stone.

In terms of the impression you want to make, you should aim to create the impact of someone who:

- is thoughtful about their performance
- is confident about their strengths (not too modest!)
- is able to be objective about their own attributes
- has learned from their experiences
- is purposeful about what they want to achieve.

Motivation questions

It is not unusual for an interviewer to ask about your motivation. In other words:

So what is it that makes you want to come and work for us?

This non-competency-based question comes up sufficiently often that it is worth planning your response in advance. As before, the best answer is an authentic one, but there are some tips that are worth bearing in mind as you prepare and answer this kind of question.

- Avoid outrageous flattery: don't say *'Because you are recognised as the best IT employer in the region'* unless it is patently true.
- Avoid what they will see as trivial motives – they will want you to signal the same interest and enthusiasm that they (hopefully) have for the business. So avoid answers like:
  > *'Well the transport routes here are really convenient for me.'*
  > *'You pay more than my current employer.'*
  > *'I'm a bit bored where I am and I fancied a change.'*
- Find some solid, positive reasons behind your application, for example:
  - a job with more scope or challenge
  - a chance to further develop your skills
  - reputation of the organisation
  - a chance to better use skills that you already have.

In general, it is better to find reasons for wanting to join that particular organisation rather than a particular profession or area of work. After all, the interviewer probably works for the organisation, and it helps if your enthusiasm validates the employment choices they have made!

Tips for self-evaluation, self-disclosure and motivation questions

■ Recognising some weaknesses or gaps in your portfolio of skills shows objectivity, but don't overdo it. If you can, show how you have recognised this deficit, what you have been doing about it and how it has improved.

■ Try to be objective in describing yourself 'on a good day' and 'on a bad day', but again, don't overdo it. Don't make any of your weaknesses sound fatal but do show how you manage them. For example *'I know I can be a bit of a perfectionist but I have learned to manage this so that I don't get hung up on detail any more'*.

■ Have at least one 'significant learning experience' up your sleeve. In other words, something that went wrong but that has left you a better person as a result. (In the Civil Service they used to say that no one got to be a Permanent Secretary without showing that they had survived – and learned from – at least one major crisis in their career.)

■ In the same way, have at least one 'significant success' available to be discussed. Analyse the situation in advance so that you can quickly describe the part you played in the success; if you can, break this down into task, thought and people and build your answer using **CAR**.

You will sometimes be asked about your ambitions or about the progression you expect to achieve. Your best guide here is to be honest; glib answers stand out like a sore thumb.

IN A NUTSHELL

Non-competency questions are hard to 'read' in terms of what they are trying to get at. Apply the same principles as you do to competency-based questions when framing your answers.

- Listen carefully and ask for clarification if you need to.
- Use **CAR** to frame your answer; describe the context, the action you took and the result in response to any question that gives you the chance to do so.
- Try to relate questions back to actual examples, where you can describe what you really did.
- Aim to be reasonably objective when asked to self-evaluate; present yourself as honest but confident in your abilities.
- Don't make things up or pretend to have knowledge or expertise when you don't; your credibility, once damaged, is extremely difficult to regain in an interview situation.

8 TROUBLESHOOTING

This chapter is all about those last things that you need to think about so as to avoid running into difficulties, as well as thinking about what can go wrong during the interview. Some may seem obvious, but it's still worth drawing your attention to them. You never know, it may remind you about something that you just haven't thought of.

No matter how well you prepare for an interview, something could still not go according to your original plan. This chapter, therefore, will provide you with some additional information that can help you during a competency-based interview. We've divided it into two broad sections:

■ before the interview

■ during the interview.

Before the interview

Being late

We've all seen the comedy programmes or heard the excuses of people being late for an interview, and whilst it doesn't make a good first impression, it's life, and sometimes people are unavoidably delayed.

You should ensure that you leave plenty of time to travel to the interview venue, so allow time for train delays or traffic jams. Better to spend 40 minutes in a café near the company's office than to arrive late.

Do ensure that you have a contact name and number before you set off, so that if the worst comes to the worst and you are unavoidably delayed you can call to let them know. At least this way you are showing that you are aware of the problem and dealing with it proactively.

Ultimately, the organisation may cancel the interview. If this happens, you should try to rearrange – in most instances they are willing to accommodate this, so long as you have been open about your reasons for being late.

How many examples should I prepare?

There are no clear answers to this, as in part it depends on the length of the interview and seniority of the role you are going for. In a 60-minute interview it is usually only possible to cover about four to five areas, with one example for each.

For a more senior level role, it is likely that several examples will be sought, as these will demonstrate a breadth of experience that is needed for the role. A good rule of thumb, therefore, is not to overuse an example from one question to the next. While it may be appropriate and show experience across different competencies, it may also indicate a lack of breadth of experience – which may count against you.

The best thing to do is to follow the guidance of the interviewer. They will structure the interview to ensure that they get the information that is necessary to make a decision. If you do need to use the same example more than once, try to think of an additional example and offer this as well – at least you are indicating that you do have others, and the interviewer may choose to explore that one with you too.

Having incorrect expectations

There are many ways in which expectations can be proved wrong – from expecting a certain room layout, to expecting certain questions to come up, or that the interviewer will have a particular style – even to what the interviewer will look like or how they will act, if you have spoken to them on the telephone before the interview. This can really throw you when you arrive and meet the interviewer, for example. It is best not to over-visualise things before the interview. It is likely to build expectations that will then not be met and may put you on the back foot, making you feel less comfortable and thus undermining your performance.

Focus on those things that you can control and prepare for realistically, ie knowing about the business, knowing the competencies and understanding as much about the interview process as you can, as well as giving good thought to potential examples.

DON'T PREPARE ANSWERS – PREPARE EXAMPLES

In our experience, one of the things most guaranteed to undermine performance during an interview is answering the question you anticipated rather than the question asked. Referring to a written, pre-prepared answer puts you at a real disadvantage here, as you then have to rethink how you can fit the prepared answer into the question that has been asked. This is difficult and is usually done in a clumsy way that undermines the quality of the response.

Don't do it!

Focus instead on identifying some broad examples that fit into the areas of task, thought and people.

How far back will they go?

Typically, in a competency-based interview the questions are not time bound. An interviewer is unlikely to focus on a particular job and ask for examples from that role. Instead, they will leave the choice of what examples and from what role to you. You would be well advised to use recent examples, as these are most likely to be of the level required for the role.

However, there may be instances in an interview where your CV is very carefully explored (see Chapter 7). Some of the financial institutions, for example, are required by FSA regulations to ensure that people really do have the experience they say they do. They'll often do this by exploring your CV and covering every single job and role you have had in your career. This type of interview is commonly called a 'chronology interview'. By definition, they will go back a long way.

During the interview

Organisationally

From an organisational perspective, the things that could go wrong are that you arrive for interview and reception are not expecting you, or the interviewer is not fully prepared. This, in our experience, is very rare. More important is to consider what could go wrong from your perspective – you have some control over this and our preparation tips should help.

Another possibility is that you are invited to meet some people in the organisation you have applied to, just to 'have a chat'. This has happened to a few people we know, and that 'chat' turns into a full-blown interview, for which the applicant has obviously not prepared. This is a difficult and unfortunate situation to have to deal with. To avoid this, as part of your preparation make sure that you find out what the 'chat' is about. If you've been told that it really is a chat, then you can feel confident in raising your lack of full preparation if it becomes something more serious than that. Better still, prepare as though it were an interview: why would you be asked in for a 'chat' if they were not seeking to evaluate you in some way?

Nerves

The most common factor affecting performance in an interview are nerves. All of us will experience a degree of anxiety before an interview, although careful preparation will minimise this. Nevertheless, you are likely to experience some tension and this is likely to show in the following ways.

- Not being completely at ease – perhaps being more formal than you usually are. This may get in the way of your establishing a rapport with the interviewer. Whilst it is partly up to the interviewer to put you at ease, you also have a role to play. Focusing on your breathing and taking slow and deep breaths before an interview will help to mitigate this. It's an approach that performers frequently use.
- Talking more quickly than you normally do – again, use your preparation to assess if this is a risk for you and whether you consciously need to slow yourself down. Our advice to people who do talk too quickly is to practise

speaking at a pace that sounds slightly too slow 'in your own head'; it is a presentation skills tip, and it works for interviews as well.

■ Nervousness can also result in clammy hands, and you will want to avoid a damp handshake! Once again, make sure you arrive in plenty of time and can therefore wash your hands before the interview. (And take the opportunity to make a final check on your appearance).

Memory

During the interview itself, your memory may let you down. You are, after all, being asked to recall things that may have happened a while ago (again, preparation is your best defence). If you cannot remember, try not to get flustered. Tell the interviewer that you need a moment to gather your thoughts – they will usually be fine with this. If you still struggle, make a note of the question and ask if you can return to it later on. Most interviewers will move on and come back at the end. Remember, it's not a memory test.

Drying up

You may find yourself drying up in the interview – both in terms of what to say as well as physically – your mouth goes dry.

The latter is easy to deal with – ensure that you have access to water.

The first is a little more difficult. There are many things going on in an interview situation. You are obviously focusing on your answers and concentrating hard. You are also being asked difficult questions, and at the same time are trying to assess the impact that your answers are having. Many people will try to second-guess what the interviewer is thinking, and it is easy to misinterpret this. For example, formality is often mistaken for a critical attitude, or that things are not going well, and this in turn can lead to your becoming anxious, with the risk that you dry up. All these thoughts are likely to impact negatively on your performance. It's important not to read too much into what the interviewer is saying or doing – they are there to do a professional job. Your role is to provide the best answers you can, so that is what you need to focus on.

Your role is to provide the best answers you can, so that is what you need to focus on.

What if I don't know the answer?

As we have seen, there are some pretty tough and searching questions in this type of interview. There are a few things to remember in terms of 'not knowing the answer'.

1. First of all, an interview is not a memory test. If you can't think of an example immediately, let the interviewer know. Tell them that you need a bit of time to gather your thoughts. A good interviewer will give you this time. If you cannot think of an example, you can always ask to come back to that question later on. If you do this, try to avoid it affecting the rest of the interview. Focus on the remaining questions, rather than trying to think of an example while answering other questions.
2. There are seldom clearly right or wrong answers, only good and less good examples. Therefore, try not to think of it as 'not knowing the answer'. The worst that can happen is that you do not have precisely relevant experience and cannot, therefore, provide a strong example. However, if you have done your preparation, if you have sought out the organisation's competencies beforehand and thought about them, the chances of this happening will be minimal.
3. If you are unsure as to whether an example is suitable, you could outline it broadly and then check with the interviewer whether that is the sort of thing they are asking for.
4. As covered in Chapter 7, you may be asked questions of a technical nature that are not competency related. These are likely to have right and wrong answers. As part of your preparation, you will need to establish what the technical components of the role will be. They are usually outlined in the job description.

They're asking me inappropriate questions

Before we get into any details, we need to be clear on what constitutes an 'inappropriate question'. There is very clear legislation in the UK and the rest of Europe so far as employment is concerned, and consequently there are some areas which may not be probed in an interview because they could open the door to unfair discrimination. Discrimination is unfair when it occurs on grounds that are not relevant to the role. The current legislation covers:

- race, nationality, ethnicity
- gender, gender reassignment
- sexual orientation
- religion or belief
- disability
- age.

The above legislation will be incorporated into the Single Equality Bill. For more information, visit the following website:

www.equalityhumanrights.com/legislative-framework/equality-bill/

CANDIDATES WITH DISABILITIES

If you have a disability you may want to let the interviewer know about it before you attend for interview, in case you have any specific requirements. For example, your interview day may also involve some form of assessment using IT, and you may need a computer with relevant software. Equally, if you have a hearing impairment, will this affect the interview? The organisation should be prepared to make reasonable adjustments for you, and it should not affect the outcome of the hiring decision. If in any doubt, seek advice beforehand from one of the organisations that provides advice about your specific disability.

Asking questions about any of the above can potentially lead to unfair discrimination and, under current legislation, should not be done. Some examples include:

'Are you planning on having any children?'

This question is sometimes asked (only by untrained interviewers), but, funnily enough, typically only of women. Thus it is potentially discriminating. You are well within your rights to say that this question has no bearing on your ability to do the job. At the same time you might worry that pointing out that it is inappropriate may damage your chances. Our view is that you should not let it go. You will need to find your own moral ground on this, but remember, the law is on your side. A potential compromise is to say, 'OK, I will answer that question, [if indeed you are willing], but you need to be aware that you shouldn't have asked it.'

'This is a full-time post, how will you manage with childcare?'

This is inappropriate again, as it is usually asked of women and opens the door to discrimination. Further, irrespective of gender, childcare arrangements should not form part of the hiring decision and should therefore not be asked about. Therefore, use our advice on the previous pages.

KNOW WHAT THE LAW SAYS

It is worth knowing the employment legislation in broad outline so that you can recognise when an inappropriate question is being asked.

A final point to make is that the burden of proof lies with an employer. This means that if you are rejected for a role and you believe that the decision has been based on unfair discrimination, then it is up to the employer to prove otherwise – one of the few cases in law where a party is guilty until proved innocent. Good employers will be aware of the legislation and will be compliant with it. They will create an audit trail of the selection process, for example interview notes, as a means of defending themselves in an instance where an appeal is made on grounds of unfair discrimination.

In terms of how you actually deal with an inappropriate question when confronted with it, there are two approaches. You can point it out at the time and explain why you are not prepared to answer, or you can answer, but keep a note of what has been asked. In the spirit of openness, we suggest indicating the inappropriateness of the question, but answering if you are prepared to. The key thing is to give thought to this before the interview, rather than being caught out on the day.

IN A NUTSHELL

Interviews will not always go as anticipated. Preparation is key and will help you in most instances. In this respect:

- In your preparation, focus on what you can control and ignore that which you can't.
- Avoid going into the interview with too many expectations.
- Think about how you will respond to possible inappropriate questions before you attend the interview.
- Remember, it's not a memory test – take control of the situation and ask for time if you need it.
- Give thought to controlling your nerves.

9 AND FINALLY...

We've covered a lot of ground in this book, our aim being to give you the best possible guidance to help you shine in a tough interview.

We've covered:

■ the nature of competencies and how organisations use them
■ how to prepare yourself
■ some shorthand ways of assessing what a questioner is getting at – 'task, thought, people'
■ some ways of building good answers – **CAR**
■ above all, examples of poor and better answers to help you to practise framing your own impressive answers.

Throughout, we have tried to distil many years of experience (as interviewers and designers of interviews) into practical tips and guidance that will help you to do your best.

We have also made the point that, all too often, we tend to think of interviews as adversarial occasions, where one party is trying to catch the other out. Indeed, in giving you all this guidance we risk falling into the trap ourselves – by implying that there are specific ways to 'outwit' an interviewer. A final piece of advice, then, is to try to get out of this mindset!

In the great majority of interview situations that you will encounter you can – and should – assume professionalism and goodwill on both sides. To do otherwise is to risk turning the occasion into a game of hide and seek, rather than a meeting where two (or more) people are exploring mutual 'fit' in terms of a potential job or role. Our guidance in this book has been focused on helping you to understand the kinds of process that interviewers use, so that you can help them to come to the best decision. Thankfully, this same guidance is also likely to enable you to present yourself in the best possible light.

Human social interaction is a highly evolved and sophisticated activity. Our ability to present ourselves well to others has evolved in parallel with our ability to detect characteristics such as trustworthiness, authenticity, credibility and so on. All of these highly developed interpersonal skills come into sharp focus in the interview situation, where the interviewer – whether explicitly or not – will be evaluating you in terms of some of these less definable characteristics, as well as in terms of specific competencies and job criteria.

Competency-based interviews – the focus of most of our examples – have been developed to help interviewers better focus on the attributes that matter, without being distracted by personal or irrelevant preferences – though, as mentioned above, it is difficult for anyone to fully 'switch off' the results of 60,000 years of social evolution! Our task has been to help you to recognise both the impression management and the more structured elements of tough interviews, and to prepare yourself accordingly.

Potentially, the greatest barrier is lack of understanding of the structured interview process and the characteristics the interviewer is looking for.

Our parting message, then, our best advice, is to be yourself – to be as authentic as you can and to use our tips to help remove any barriers that may prevent the interviewer from seeing you as the talented and valuable prospective employee that you are! Potentially, the greatest barrier is simple lack of understanding of the structured interview process and the characteristics that the interviewer is looking for. Armed with the information in this book you should be well prepared to avoid the barriers and ensure that the real you has the best chance of coming through at an interview. Coming through in a way that is professional and human helps the interviewer to see you at your best – and gives you the best chance of getting the job you want.

Good luck!